ALSO BY SHONI LABOWITZ

Miraculous Living

God, Sex and Women of the Bible

DISCOVERING OUR SENSUAL, SPIRITUAL SELVES

SHONI LABOWITZ

Simon & Schuster

SIMON & SCHUSTER
Rockefeller Center
1230 Avenue of the Americas
New York, NY 10020

Simon & Schuster and colophon are registered trademarks of Simon & Schuster, Inc.

Designed by Jeanette Olender
Manufactured in the United States of America

10 9 8 7 6 5 4 3 2 1

Library of Congress Cataloging-in-Publication Data
Labowitz, Shoni.
God, Sex and Women of the Bible: discovering our sensual,
spiritual selves / Shoni Labowitz.
p. cm.
Includes bibliographical references (p. 249) and index.
1. Women in the Bible.   2. Bible. O.T.—Feminist criticism.
3. Bible and feminism   4. Sex in the Bible.
5. Feminist spirituality   6. Feminism—Religious aspects—Judaism.
7. Judaism—Doctrines.   I. Title.
BS575.L33 1998
221.9'22'082—dc21   98-23304 CIP
ISBN 0-684-83717-X

Dedicated to my dearly beloved mother,

Rebbetzin Nechama Rabinowitz Leibowitz,

of blessed memory, a woman of faith, courage and dignity,

and to the modern-day goddess

in whose motherly care she entrusted my spirit,

Florence Molomut Ross,

my mentor and dearest friend.

Acknowledgments

A book like this is a compilation of many voices. I am grateful for the innumerable voices of God that came to me through the words of the Bible and the women who have shared their stories, particularly those in the Temple Adath Or spirituality group. I am especially grateful to Dee Fuller for the care and time spent transcribing those stories and to Cheyenne Chernov for continuing to provide the forum in which women of all faiths and backgrounds can share their truths.

I would also like to thank Florence Ross, Nola Firestone, Lisa Crane and Dr. Lisa Sirota Weiner, for reading and responding to the chapters as they were unfolding; Dr. Donald E. Riggs, Vice President for Information Services and University Librarian at the Einstein Library of Nova Southeastern University, for his assistance in helping me locate many of the resources cited in this book; Rabbi Zalman Schachter-Shalomi, Founder of P'nai Or Fellowship and Professor at Nairopa Institute, for being my spiritual mentor and dear friend for whom no question was too large or small; Rabbi Bernard Pressler, for his generosity in sharing

ACKNOWLEDGMENTS

his electronic library; Edith Gordon, of blessed memory, and her husband, Manuel, and daughter, Bonnie Gordon, for providing the home in which I write; Howard Chess, Executive Director of Temple Adath Or, for his wisdom, friendship and devotion; the Temple Adath Or community, for their loving support; Irene Greene, for her patience and administrative assistance; Tanya Russo and Caryn Farrell, for their continuous encouragement and advice; John Brockman, for professional guidance; Mary Ann Naples, for believing in the message of this book; Carlene Bauer, for the profound conversations that enhanced the editing process; Andrew Jakabovics, for his spiritual openness in copy editing; Fred Hills, for championing a new book; my family, Marc, Arik, David, Pierre, Christina, Marina and Melissa, for their unconditional love; and, most importantly, my soul mate Phillip, for sharing my passion for God, life and spirituality.

Contents

11

Introduction

When a woman speaks her truth, it is as holy as prayer. At times the truth of another touches us so profoundly that it is a life-changing experience. It is with this form of prayer I welcome you into this book, where you can come to know the truth about yourself and your relationship with God. It connects women to a rich and vibrant feminine tradition of sexuality and spirituality. Through exploring the inner lives and desires of eight biblical women and their goddess ancestry, you will discover the mysteries that reside in all women and understand that your life is part of a much larger story—one you were never told.

Did you ever read the Bible and wonder why Eve was considered evil and God was a man? What was so terrible about Eve's sin that God closed down paradise and blamed Eve for the beginning of pain and death in the world? Did this mean that all females are as sinful as Eve and all men as powerful and blameless as God? Or did you ever wonder why God created the world with the Garden of Eden and then destroyed it in Noah's flood? The rabbis, priests and scholars of old found their answers in the biblical text. They concluded that God did not destroy the world; rather, it was human weakness that destroyed the world and it all started in the Garden of Eden with Eve's sin. They explained that because Eve, the archetypal female, ate the fruit of the forbidden tree, she brought male domination, death and pain into the world.

This kind of indoctrination caused deep wounds to woman's self-image that have lasted for centuries until now. The image of God as a jealous, punishing parent intimidated women, inhibiting their sexuality and creativity. This intimidation drove many a woman into a lifestyle dominated by ecclesiastical rules and regulations that left little room for creative individuality. According to the old biblical interpretations, God by way of the Bible was telling us that if we were to do our part in healing the pain of this world, we had to subjugate our sexuality and diminish our individuality. This message of intimidation and subjugation does not speak to the women of today. No wonder so many women in my group knew so little about the Bible, and those who knew more felt alienated from it. When stories exclude our voices and are alien to our experience as modern women, we lose interest.

Coming to terms with my own alienation laid the foundation for this book. It started in 1979, eight years before I was ordained or even gave thought to becoming a rabbi and sharing my insights with thousands of other women. I led a prayer group of women of varying ages and religious backgrounds that gathered each Saturday morning in a circle on my living room floor. These women claimed to know little about their own religious traditions and even less about the Bible. They looked to me for guidance in navigating through the biblical stories in ways that would touch their souls. I was in a quandary.

How could I share teachings from a book about which I had more questions than answers? For centuries people have studied the Bible, exploring their own truths. Who are we? Why are we here? Why is a particular thing happening? Why is it happening to us? Why now? How can we help heal ourselves and others? With each answer came more questions. Such answers as I had came from the rabbis of old, and they were not the kind of answers that spoke to my soul. To teach the Bible I had to love and feel passionate about the Bible, and as a woman with an awakening consciousness, it was difficult to espouse a doctrine that was seemingly void of women's experience. I needed help.

I fervently believe the cliché that when we ask for guidance, guidance comes. My guidance came in the form of two spiritual encounters, first in a dream and then in a coincidence. In the dream I was embraced by the presence of an ethereal being. She enveloped my body with a reverberating sound like that of *aleph*, the first letter of the Hebrew alphabet, the sound that the Israelites heard when they stood at the foot of Mount Sinai to receive the Ten Commandments. The *aleph* has substance, but no sound, yet within it are the possibilities of all sounds, like the color white, which holds the possibilities of all colors. Surrounded by the white noise, I had the sensation of being handed the silenced voice of woman, a silence that was passed from generation to generation. A silence that struggled like a scream to be freed. This ethereal being was empowering me to break the silence of woman's voice by retranslating Torah. I awoke from the dream feeling excited, yet inadequate and confused. Even though I had spent my childhood, graduate and postgraduate years steeped in Bible study, who was I to think that I could retranslate the Hebrew Bible? Especially since I had not yet learned all there is to know! I was dumbfounded to think that I could even attempt such a project.

Then, doing what I do best when I get nervous, I started cleaning the closets. I was carefully emptying a top shelf to wash it down when a paper fluttered out of nowhere. It was a college term paper my mother had written. I had no idea my mother wrote a paper entitled "A Psychoanalytical Viewpoint of the Bible" and I certainly did not know I had it in my home, much less in the closet, buried between the terry towels and embroidered napkins. Opening to the first page, I read her argument for the importance of reinterpreting the Bible according to one's emotional needs and relevant circumstances. In citing Dr. Dorothy Zelig's book *Psychoanalysis and the Bible,* my mother wrote, "in order to find new meanings . . . one must start with the mind as a tabula rasa. . . ."

I put down the washrag, moved the water bucket aside and slid down the wall to the floor. Start with my mind as a tabula rasa! This was as clear a message as I could get. I did not need to be an itinerant scholar. I only needed to empty my mind of old programming and be willing to see the text with fresh eyes, to give God's Book a chance to speak to me as though I am hearing it for the first time. Then I could retranslate and reinterpret the Bible according to my own truth as a woman and as a human being.

THE BIBLE: A TEXT BOTH ENDURING AND EVOLVING

The purpose of the Bible is to bring us closer to God. The Gaon of Vilna said that everything that ever was, is and will be, is written into the Bible. The Zohar, the kabbalistic Book of Splendor, says that God and the Bible are one.[1] Kabbalah teaches that God gives the Bible to the people as a bridegroom would give a wedding contract to his bride. If the Bible is indeed God's wedding contract to us, and if it includes everything that ever was, is and will be, then our deepest yearnings, desires, hopes and dreams must be written into these ancient yet timeless passages.

The Hebrew Bible is called Tanakh, which is an acronym for the Torah (Five Books of Moses), Nevi'im (Prophets) and Ketuvim (Writings). The Torah, which is divided into weekly readings, is the part of the Bible most often read. Did you ever see an original Torah scroll? On white parchment the Hebrew words—without vowels—are inscribed by hand. Without vowels the Hebrew letters are just black shapes on white parchment. To give the letters sound, we give them vowels, which determine the translation and interpretation of the word. Rabbi Moses ben Nachman, known as Nachmanides, once wrote that the relationship between the literal words and their interpretation can be compared to the relationship between the consonants and vowels of the Torah. What Nachmanides meant to show was that the words do not speak until we give them sounds; therefore the black shapes on white parchment do not really exist on their own until we bring the commentary to them. In other words, he understood that the interpretation of the text needs to be relevant to the circumstances of our lives, and the circumstances of our lives are always changing.

It is through the Bible that we discover what is in the Bible. Unless we are confronted with the word, unless we

continue our dialogue with the Prophets, unless we respond,
the Bible ceases to be Scripture.

A. J. Heschel[2]

When I opened the pages as if for the very first time, what I found in the Bible was that the Hebrew text itself does not denigrate women. Only certain ways in which the text has been interpreted does. How we choose to see ourselves in the Bible depends on how we choose to interpret the Hebrew text and translate it from the original Hebrew into English. Each word in Hebrew has a root form, and depending on this root and the vowels used, the word can have several different definitions. The Hebrew word spelled *aleph, shin, hey,* depending upon which vowels are placed under the letters, could be translated as either "sacrifice" or "woman." Throughout history, some have unwittingly confused these two meanings without knowing the Hebrew— consider Joan of Arc, the Salem witch trials. We can now reinterpret and reframe the old perceptions of what sacrifice implies for any life-form, and reappropriate the place of woman from that of a thing expendable, to the sacred living passion of God.

Another example is the word *mara,* used to refer to both Miriam and Naomi, two women whose lives you will enter in the pages of this book. *Mara,* the Hebrew root word in Miriam—has traditionally been translated to mean "bitter." However, Miriam and *mara* come from the letters *mem, resh,* and *aleph,* and those same letters can mean "fly, soar, or rise."[3] In chapter 6, we will see that Numbers 12 tells the story of Miriam speaking with Moses about his wife, Zipporah. This has traditionally been translated as Miriam speaking against Moses and his nuptial relationship. The rabbis of old said that Miriam was stricken with leprosy following that incident because, true to her name, she was embittered with arrogance and false pride. However, in retranslating the word *miriam,* we find that instead of being bitter, Miriam was rising up like a new wave of understanding, especially when it came to the needs of women like her sister-in-law, Zipporah.

Then in the Book of Ruth, we read about Naomi and Ruth. Naomi is returning home after a long absence and tells the people to call her Mara instead of Naomi. Since *mara* is traditionally translated as "the embittered one," the rabbis said that she returned embittered by her past failures. Yet *mara,* as we found in the word *miriam,* can also be translated as "the one who rises above difficulties." Naomi could have been telling the people that she was overcoming the challenges of her past and ascending to the next level of her spiritual development. The difference between bitter and rising is enough to change the images of these women from one that is negative to one that is positive.

The biblical text is not just relating one story at one time in one way, but instead is a timeless tale that is part of the whole context of a greater story of humanity. Each word holds a possibility of sounds, shapes and nuances that can cross cultures, religions, continents and time itself. For example, let us look at the word *Elohim* in Genesis 1:1. "In the beginning God [Elohim] created the heaven and the earth." *Elohim* has traditionally been translated to mean "God," but if you look at the composition of the word, the root form is *Eloha,* meaning "one God." *Elohim* is the plural for *Eloha.* If the biblical text used *Eloha* instead of *Elohim,* we would be sure it was referring to one God. However, with the word *Elohim,* it could imply many gods. Though the word *Elohim* appears to be plural in Hebrew, it takes a singular verb. Perhaps the Bible is telling us that this one God manifests in many different forms. What is interesting is that when we go back to the word *Eloha,* we hear it echoed in other languages, other times. There is El amongst the Canaanites; Elohim amongst the Jews; Allah amongst the Arabs; Haloha, the festival of the Gods, amongst the Greeks and Angles; Heloha, the female deity, amongst the Native Americans. The echo remains in *aloha,* the greeting of Hawaiians, and "hello," the greeting of Americans.[4] Perhaps it is no coincidence that the Zohar says, "Welcoming a person with a greeting of peace and harmony is akin to welcoming God."[5]

Words, peoples, cultures and religions do not exist in isolation. Somewhere in the vast information available in the words of the Bible we can find ourselves as women. And when we do we recognize that God is an unconditionally loving God who not only created one people and one tradition, but created the possibility for many peoples and many traditions. Through exploring the Bible with fresh eyes we are able to cross the boundaries of time and to touch ancient cultures while gleaning meaningful insights for our own lives.

REINTERPRETATION: A GIFT FROM GOD

Along with translating the Hebrew text in the Bible, there is what the rabbis call "reading the spaces in between the words." Anyone can read the literal words on a page. But the women and men who can interpret the unspoken words that are the spaces in the text can see within these stories a mirror image of themselves. It is like reading a letter from a friend. Anyone can read the letter and collect the information, but only one who is intimate with the writer or the message behind the words can ascertain whether the written expressions are angry or loving, serious or witty. In the same way, the Bible is not a static series of cut-and-dried verses that are relics from an ancient past. It is dynamic, organic and ever-growing new ways of thinking that prompt us to experience the full range of human emotions and then enable us to see the irony and humor in our own lives. The Bible depends on our willingness to laugh, cry and be open in order to show us the humor, pathos and sensuality of its stories and teachings. Only the reader who is willing to be intimate and dive into the text can explore the possibilities in the spaces between the words for new revelations and broader insights. This is why the blessing that we say before studying the Bible is: "Blessed are You, Holy One of the Universe, who has guided us to immerse ourselves in the words of Torah." This immersion into the words and exploration of the spaces in between the words that leads to new interpretations is called midrash.

Midrashic exegesis dates back to 400 C.E. and comprises a large part of rabbinic literature.[6] The method of midrashic exegesis is embodied by the Hebrew word *pardes. Pardes* sounds like the English word *paradise* and literally means "a garden of pleasure." It is symbolic of the spiritual state one enters while contemplating the possible meanings of Bible text. *Pardes* is an acronym for four words that indicate the four levels of midrash. They are *p'shat,* the literal level; *remez,* the symbolic meaning of the literal level; *d'rash,* the inquiry between the *p'shat* and *remez;* and finally *sod,* the hidden spiritual message that relates directly to the person or people interpreting the text. With this method of understanding we read a Bible verse and ask: (1) What are the words literally saying? (2) What are these words implying symbolically? (3) What do we learn from the simple and implied meanings of the verse? And finally, each person asks her- or himself (4) What is the hidden message that can help me in my life now?

When people innovate new ideas in Torah, they are creating jewels for the Divine Presence.

Rabbi Zecharia Mendel of Yereslov[7]

Retranslating and reinterpreting is a part of Jewish tradition and has been going on for more than two thousand years. The Hebrew Bible is a compilation of sacred stories, priestly rituals and guides for living handed from generation to generation. These stories have been edited, expanded and molded into holy literature that fits the belief system of the time. Each generation interprets the text in ways that are relevant to its emotional and spiritual needs and builds upon the commentaries of the previous ones. The Bible, in part or as a whole, has been translated into most languages and dialects, each translation biased according to a particular culture. For example, in the late biblical period there were rabbis who translated the Bible from Hebrew into Aramaic; they are known as the *m'targ'mim,* or "translators." The *m'targ'mim* brought a sense of freedom to their Aramaic renditions, embellishing some passages and avoiding others in order to highlight a moral or theological issue.

We diminish the possibility that God's Book can bring to our lives when we stop the words from dancing off the pages into our spirits. Rabbi Levi Yitzchak of Berditchev said that the Bible was given to the people so that each generation could come to God on their own, in innovative ways.[8] Each new idea we glean from the biblical text becomes our gift to God. In Deuteronomy 10:16, through Moses, God instructs each person who wants to connect in a Godly way, to "circumcise the foreskin of your heart." We can see the foreskin as a symbol of a filter we place on ourselves that keeps us stubbornly attached to old ideas and old ways of being, even if they no longer fit our present circumstances. I believe God is guiding us to circumcise the foreskins of our hearts, because God wants us to fold back that which limits us from thinking bigger thoughts and speaking deeper truths that are relevant to our newly changing physical and emotional lives. Each person's heart needs to voice her or his own experience. We are not rubber stamps of each other, nor standardized models of our culture, but uniquely divine imprints of God. If we keep folding back our limitations to uncover the Bible's wisdom, we give ourselves an opportunity to come closer to knowing who God is in us and making God an integral part of our lives.

THE STORIES: A MAP TO RETRIEVE LOST VOICES AND HIDDEN PASSIONS

In this book I want to give voice to the truth of woman as I have translated it from the Bible, heard it from the women in my groups and lived it in my own life. Through my own intuition I have taken the liberty to enhance descriptions in ways that validate women's experiences, and in many cases I have found plausible sources in biblical, kabbalistic, mythological and anthropological scholarly texts to justify the interpretations. For the most part, the translations of the Hebrew text are my own—unless otherwise cited—in order to bring out the linguistic nuances that helped me to new insights.

In grounding women's voices in biblical text, my intention is not to change history but to redefine and reinterpret the text to become more meaningful to the women of today and the daughters of tomorrow. Like the rabbis of old, and

INTRODUCTION

in the tradition of the *m'targ'mim* and midrashim, there are times when I have referred to the whole and other times when I have used only parts of stories or segments of sentences. Many times I felt like a miner searching for the diamonds in a dark tunnel of texts and verses. I mined only the jewels that I felt enhanced our images as women, without taking from any other life-form. Every once in a while there would be a nagging, skeptical inner voice that said, "Shoni, give it up. What are you trying to do? Put a new dress on an old mannequin and make it fit?" But I remembered my spiritual encounter with the silent scream and "started with the mind as a tabula rasa."

As I have continued researching, studying and dreaming these stories for the past twenty years, too many synchronicities have occurred for me to assume that I was on the wrong track, or alone in this search. I lived these archetypes and they lived me. Books and teachers would inexplicably appear to lead me to other books and other teachers, all of which gave me information that verified and validated my quest. There were nights when I was awakened by dreams that led me to just the right book and exact page that would open my mind to more curiosity and more realizations. I am thankful for the instruments that have guided me in seeing things in a new way, all the while honoring the sacredness of the holy words of the original text.

27

INTRODUCTION

For every part in your body and in your life, there is a parallel part in the many faces of God.

Tikkunei Zohar, 69:100b, 130b

If we are open to it, the Bible can be a map to the sacred mysteries of a woman's pleasure and passion. The Baal Shem Tov, founder of Hasidism, taught that love is a godly attribute. He said erotic, sexual passions are in us in order to love God. Kabbalah describes everything about life in images of perpetual sexual interplay. Just as Kabbalah teaches that physical union should be pleasurable, and in it one should feel vibrant and joyous, so too in speaking words of Torah, for Torah is God's wedding vow to each person. Passion for God is good and passion for God is lived through our relationships on earth.

As women we want to feel a presence of God within ourselves and to be able to see ourselves in the feminine images of God. We want to acknowledge that for more than twenty-five thousand years previous to the Bible there was a goddess-based matriarchal society in which God was a woman, nature was sacred, people lived peacefully and women were the leaders in religious and social life. In the following pages you will hear women's voices sharing with you what they have come to know, through God and the

28

Bible, about themselves as women. In their growing intimacy with God they have become more loving and intimate with themselves. Through the voices that are both ancient and new, we learn not only that the Bible is our wedding contract with God, but that when we touch our bodies, we touch God; when we pleasure ourselves, we pleasure God; when we shed blood, we shed the blood of God; when we are in union with another, we are in union with God; when we birth new life, we birth new forms of God; and as our bodies change, our image of God changes.

For a woman to know that her body is beautiful and sex is sacred is not enough. We need to feel the visceral passion of this beauty and sanctity. We want to have the joy of this passion color everything we think, say and do. And we want this passion to lift us up as we walk, dance and, sometimes, stumble through our lives. Then we will feel alive and vibrant.

With each chapter, this book explores the different stages of life that affect a woman's sexuality. We see Leah, Rachel, Eve, Jochebed, Deborah, Miriam, Naomi and other women of the Bible step off the pages to guide us from self-discovery to confident maturity, from menstruation to menopause. Their stories of vulnerability and courage provide catalysts for diving deep into the soul of woman and turning the silent scream to a melody.

From outward appearances, little seems to change in our

lives. Oh yes, we add some wrinkles and maybe some pounds over the years. Yet the really significant changes that occur are the paths we choose to take that give us a better understanding of who we are, why we are here and where we are going. In writing this book I have chosen to take new roads to get us to an old place, one resplendent with the heartfelt knowledge of previous generations. It has been an awesome journey, and I have loved every moment of immersion into the words of the Bible. I felt as if the women of the past were supporting these explorations of their lives and helped give voice to their silence, which put me in mind of something Nachmanides once said: "If a person is filled with love and awe while studying Torah, that person can be certain that it is being accepted by God."

As you read this book, I pray that it gives you the confidence to know that your truth is part of God's truth. May the information that you gain in the following pages give you greater confidence to speak your truth, to live as a sexual being, to know that your sexuality is sacred and to be able to share this knowledge with women and men everywhere.

Chapter 1

Leah

FROM A PLAIN GIRL TO A NOBLE BEING

*L*aban had two daughters. His older daughter, Leah, was "weak eyed" and homely, while the younger daughter, Rachel, was beautiful and sparkling. Their cousin Jacob came to live with them, and he immediately fell in love with Rachel. Laban agreed to let Jacob marry her if he worked on Laban's property for seven years. After the seventh year, Jacob was ready to marry Rachel, but Laban was eager to rid himself of Leah. Since it was the custom that the older daughter married before the younger one, and a groom did not see his wife until after the marriage vows were completed, Laban was able to place Leah under the bridal canopy in Rachel's stead. When Jacob realized this deception, he despised Leah and was furious at Laban. Then Laban made a new deal with Jacob: He could have Rachel as his wife after the first week of consummated marriage with Leah, in exchange for another seven years labor. Leah and Rachel, along with their maidservants Bilhah and Zilpah, birthed the twelve sons who became the twelve tribes of Israel.[1]

Leah's eyes were weak, but Rachel was of beautiful form and fair to look at.

Genesis 29:17

Jacob loved Rachel more than Leah.

Genesis 29:30

SHE JUST passed by, and you did not even notice her.

But do not be concerned. She did not notice you either. She is the one with the shapeless body and mousy brown hair. See her winding her way through the courtyard maze of frolicking women and clamoring children? Over there. Her eyes possess a scrutinizing gaze that lets you know she is otherwise occupied. Can you blame her? She is the daughter of Laban, an unsavory widower who, anxious to rid himself of her, deceived Jacob, her sister's fiancé, into marrying her. Now she and her beautiful sister share the same husband. What with a father who cannot be bothered with her, a husband who despised her from the moment he was tricked into marrying her and a sister who is so much more beloved than she, the poor woman has more than you would wish to handle.

Yet don't let her appearance mislead you, for you cannot measure the heart of a woman by the features of her face, the curves on her body or the man with whom she lives. To know a woman you must peer into her heart and gently unveil her spirit. Take another look at her. Outside she is no beauty. But inside she is a goddess, a passionate woman in the throes of discovering herself. Know her intimately and you will begin to feel a vivid, shimmering sensuality, and you will wonder: What is sparking her spirit? How can she be so impoverished on one hand, and so richly blessed on the other? Who *is* this woman?

This woman is a flower coming to full bloom. They call her Leah, a name that has traditionally been interpreted to mean "one who is weary." The Bible translators read Leah to be a lackluster, weary woman who was an encumbrance to her family. They implied that her only redeeming virtue was that she was fertile and gave birth to many children. Indeed, given Leah's family history, she had every reason to be weary from her circumstances. Her problems might have whittled her down into a disempowered woman, one competing with her sister Rachel and wallowing in self-pity. Though *lamed, aleph,* and *hey,* the root letters that spell *Leah,* can mean "tired" or "heavy," they can also be translated to mean "to labor in vain" or "one who perseveres against the odds."[2] In spite of her limitations and frustrations, Leah became a testament to persevering against the odds in order to become mistress over her own body and shaper of her own life. Join me as we unveil the source of Leah's sensuality and uncover our own.

God saw that Leah was hated and God opened her womb . . .

Genesis 29:31

Who loved Leah? Not her husband, not her father, and only rarely her sister. The secret to her inner beauty was that she had a love affair with herself. This is not narcissistic, this is confidence. And every woman should have it. So often I hear women who want love talk about looking for it in a lover outside of themselves rather than from the lover within. Not Leah. She unabashedly expressed her passion, as we can see in the story of the mandrakes.[3]

On a lazy afternoon, when Leah and Rachel were relaxing in their tent, Leah's son Reuben returned from the wheat field and presented his mother with a cluster of mandrakes. These plants, called *dudaim* in Hebrew, meaning "lovers," were also known as "phallus of the fields." They were a highly prized aphrodisiac, for, unlike most vegetation, they were not easily obtainable, because they were difficult to uproot from the earth. When Rachel saw Reuben with the herbs, she appealed to Leah, saying, "Please give me [some] from your son's mandrakes." Instead of giving Rachel *some* of the mandrakes, Leah gave her *all* the mandrakes in exchange for spending that night with Jacob. This was a gamble—Leah knew full well Jacob would have preferred Rachel—but Leah had confidence in herself, in her sexuality, and went out into the field that night to meet Jacob on his way home. This was something Rachel never did.[4] Rachel would sit at home and wait for Jacob to come to her, but Leah met Jacob halfway. And when she greeted Jacob, she did not nag or manipulate, she simply said, "Come to me, you are my gift. . . ." (Genesis 30:16) Leah spoke to Jacob in the field that evening with a voice of passion that transcended their union and touched a source greater than either one of them. Her voice expressed a desire to love herself by loving Jacob, to touch God within herself by touching Jacob. In giving her sister the mandrakes, Leah was asserting a belief in herself and her own potential as a sexual being. In loving Jacob, she was connecting with the Divine spark within herself that was uniquely hers to kindle and no one else's to extinguish. When we live in the fullness of our passion, like Leah, we become more powerful and joyous.

We each live lives that are both physical and spiritual; heavenly and earthly; literal and metaphoric. Within each woman there is a plain girl and a noble being. When we treat the plain girl as a noble being our ordinary realities can become extraordinary opportunities. As one woman in my spirituality group once remarked, "I don't *just* get dressed, I anoint and adorn myself." Everything Leah did conveyed the attitude of a goddess, one determined to connect with God in her mind, body and soul.

Similarly, the choices we make determine the delicate interplay between who we are physically and who we think we are spiritually. When we begin viewing ourselves as more than just physical beings, and our lives as more than just literal existences but also as opportunities for connecting with God and bringing a little of heaven to earth, we contribute meaning to our world, even if we are just anointing and adorning ourselves. If we limit our experiences to either one dimension or the other, we are liable to miss the Divine.

Leah's sexual exploration was an integral part of her connection with the Divine power in the universe. If she, like ourselves, separated her sense of God from her physical being, her body would have been merely a tool for masturbation or baby making. Instead, when Leah connected with God in all parts of her body, she knew God as intimately as she knew herself. The God that Leah knew opened wombs, sent angels to arouse people[5] and was a sexual being, both male and female. This God was her friend, her lover, gave her seed and aided her birth into new ways of being.[6]

Traditional Bible commentaries explain that the names Leah chose for her children were an attempt to get Jacob's love and attention. They say that in naming her first son

38

Reuben she was crying out "[Jacob] see my struggle"; with the second son, Simeon, it was "[Jacob] hear me"; and with Levi, the third son, she was to entreating Jacob to join her, and so on. This interpretation is disempowering to Leah and to all women. Leah knew the power of the Divine creative force flowing through her body and partnered God in bringing that power to earth.

As Leah was birthing children, she was also birthing her sense of self-worth and initiating an intimate union with the Divine. We can see Leah naming her offspring as naming the stages and sensations of her growing intimacy and continuing dialogue with God.[7] Nearly single-handedly, she gave birth to the twelve tribes of Israel, which we see echoed in the twelve houses of the Mesopotamian moon goddess Asherah, the twelve signs of the zodiac and the twelve months of the year. As a result, Leah has had a lasting, far-reaching effect on culture.

With the first child, Reuben, she recognized the compassion with which "God saw" her intention and struggle to "build"[8] strength within. After the birth of Simeon, she felt stronger and declared, "God hears me." In Levi, she felt the harmony of "God joining" her. It was with this son that Israel's priesthood was born; this tribe of Israel dedicated themselves to bond with God through serving humanity. With the birth of the fourth son, Judah, Leah experienced an inner sense of satisfaction and success, so she "praised

God" and started a new dimension of communication with the Hebrew God: praising.[9] The Talmud says that Leah was the first person since the creation of the world to verbally express praise and gratitude to God.[10] With praise comes glory, and perhaps Leah was feeling the glory of God in her body when she birthed her fifth child and called him Issachar, or "God's reward." Her reward from God lay not in material wealth, but in the satisfaction of discovering herself. Increasingly comfortable in this knowledge, Leah named her sixth son Zebulun, declaring that "God dwells with me."

The seventh child was her hoped-for daughter, whom she named Dinah, "defender," perhaps hoping that she would be the protector of a woman's legacy in an increasingly patriarchal period. As Leah's seventh and final child, Dinah is significant in both traditions in which Leah lived: the ancient matriarchal culture of Mesopotamia, which revered women as goddesses incarnate,[11] and the early Israelite, which revered an invisible God whose glory filled every aspect of the universe and every part of human life. In the ancient matriarchal culture, Leah was the title given to the goddess known as the Wild Cow,[12] called the Seven Hathors in Egypt, for she possessed the seven planetary spirits. In the Jewish tradition, the Zohar explains that there are seven planets, corresponding to the seven firmaments that regulate the connections between the heavens and the earth.[13] In India this sacred cow, Visvarupa, is called the Golden Womb, and when a person wants to be reborn, or initiated into a religious order, or to rectify old behaviors, they perform a ritual in which, symbolically, they immerse themselves in a cowlike womb.[14]

According to the Jewish tradition, the Talmud says that when Leah was carrying her seventh child, she understood that amongst her sister, their maidservants and herself, they were destined to birth a total of twelve sons. The rabbis also implied that having a daughter diminished her power and explained that the seventh fetus in Leah's womb was supposed to have been a boy, but during her pregnancy the gender of the fetus changed and became a girl.[15]

Instead, having a daughter insured Leah's legacy. Leah's prayer was for her daughter to remember the mysteries of sensuality, sexuality and spirituality handed from generation to generation of women. Her hopes may have been encouraged by the fact that seven in both traditions is symbolic of the Sabbath, the seventh day of the week. Kabbalah teaches that the seventh day of the week is in a heightened category all to itself. The Sabbath is called "moon day" and is considered more relaxed, carefree, joyous and feminine than the other six days of the week. It is the day when the world pauses and reflects on the celestial light.[16] But this is not the end to Leah's journey, only another turn in the ascending spiral.[17]

Leah transformed a common existence into a sacred celebration of life. She moved beyond her second-class status and the petty skirmishes of her family life, to endow her life with meaning and purpose, as she created a new language of praise among people and a new nation within Israel. It is from the seed of Leah that generations later Moses is born to remind the people of the possibilities of freedom.[18]

Leah instinctively knew what many of us have forgotten—that our bodies are a source of mystery and power. Both Mesopotamian and Israelite cultures integrated spirituality with sexuality and honored the body as a temple for the Divine. Kabbalah teaches that the Divine manifests in our bodies through various metaphors. Rabbi Isaac Luria, the famous kabbalist, explained that when God was incarnated in the metaphoric image of a lover, Leah was called God's "small face." She was the archetype for the Divine body, from the feet to the heart.[19] Leah's body from her feet to her heart, like ours, not only was created in the image of God, but was an expression of all that is Godly. She knew that the more familiar she became with her body, the closer she felt to God and the more comfortable she was in her life. Leah did not have the guilt, shame or confusion about pleasure and sex that the women of today do. As we have seen, for a woman of her time, sex and religion were intimately related and probably inseparable.[20] Many spiritual masters in different traditions have taught that the path to knowing the inner spiritual mysteries begins with knowing your physical self fully, and we see this in other traditions. In oriental mythology the sexual organs were compared to the soma fruit of the moon goddess tree, in Indian mythology they were compared to the thousand-petaled flower of the lotus goddess and according to mystical Judaism they were compared to the fruit of creativity on the kabbalistic Tree of Life.

Yet most of us, at one time or another, struggle with poor body image. Our breasts are too large or too small, our thighs ripple, our arms sag or our stomachs balloon. I rarely hear a woman complain about her clitoris being too big, too small, too floppy or too tight. Come to think of it, I rarely hear women talk about their sexual parts at all! Maybe that's because most women have yet to explore their own genitals. We have taken the sexual parts of ourselves and our bodies and placed them in a closet behind a closed door. We treat our genitals like untouchables we are afraid to explore. To many women, touching their genitals is like getting caught opening someone else's treasure chest. As though their genitals are not their own. Not only are they yours, they are the most unique part of your anatomy.

I recall a young friend who confided in me that she was distraught over an illness that prevented her from taking birth control pills. She was in a relationship with a young man and was eager to maintain her sexual activity without risking pregnancy. When I mentioned other forms of prevention, she winced in discomfort and admitted it would be embarrassing to have to touch her *genitals.* This did not surprise me. Statistics tell us that over half of the nation's teenagers are sexually active and the average age when they have intercourse for the first time is between fifteen and sixteen. Yet most girls, like my young friend, have never touched, seen or explored the areas of their bodies that they allow their boyfriends to fondle.

Since she had never explored her own body, I suggested she do so in the privacy of her own room, as a sacred ritual she could perform in order to touch the beauty with which God created her. I encouraged her to see and feel what she allows another to see and feel but has closed her own eyes to. Women of all ages, I told her, have passed on the ritual of self-exploration as an initiation into sacred sensuality, and she could have a part in this. Befriending her body was befriending the miracle of who she was.

Before she left my office to explore on her own, I told her about Leah. I described how the Midrash says that Leah lived as a priestess[21] with her family in Haran, which was in the same area thought to be the birthplace of the moon goddess known as Asherah or Astarte in Mesopotamia and Canaan, Ishtar in Babylonia and Isis in Greece.[22] Like the matriarchs Sarah and Rebekah before her, Leah was one of a family of priestesses who served in the moon goddess tradition.[23] In Genesis 30:13, at the birth of her son Asher, there is indication that Leah invoked the goddess Asherah in her declaration, *"B'ashri ki ishruni banot."* This statement is translated as, "I am happy! For the daughters will call me happy" (Genesis 30:13).[24] Since the root letters for Asherah in Hebrew could mean either "happy" or "that which is," Leah could have been saying, "I am Asherah [or: Asherah is in me], for the Asherah that is in me is in all the daughters."

In helping my friend open up to the possibilities of connecting to the Divine within herself, I continued to explain that perhaps Leah's personal identification with Asherah as "I am Happy" and "that which is" laid the foundation for, centuries later, a similar translation when Moses saw the burning bush and heard God's voice in it. Moses asked God, "What is your name?" God answered, *"Eheyeh Asher Eheyeh"* (Exodus 3:14). This was a loaded statement that could be translated in numerous ways; the most popular translation is "I Am That I Am"; or to render more exactly to the Hebrew verb *eheyeh,* "I Am That Which I Am Becoming"; or to translate with a matriarchal twist, "I am Asher [the male equivalent of Asherah], I am"; or simply "I Am Happy, I Am,"[25] implying a joyous God rather than the angry, jealous God so often portrayed by the Bible translators. Even the word used for angry in Hebrew, *vayitaber* in Deuteronomy 3:26, has the same root letters as "one who passes over," and *hitanaf* in Deuteronomy 4:21 has the same root letters as "an eagle," *anafah*.[26] So that the statement used to say "God was angry" could also be interpreted to mean "God soared like an eagle." This is more akin to the kabbalistic metaphor of God as one who soars with us on the wings of an eagle, a happy God that lifts us on the wings of an eagle, one that is connected to matriarchal mythology.

When Leah explored her body, she affirmed who God was in her, and with every "I Am" statement she recognized her part in God. If she had succumbed to outside influences, like many of us do, she would have looked at her body and said, "I am fat," or "I am ugly, dirty or smelly," thereby discounting the God who was to be called "I Am That I Am" in her. Instead, Leah inspired confidence; as the Midrash says, "all who came near her felt her joy and rejoiced."[27] But self-discovery is not just for the young, like my friend. Grown-up women, especially, have forgotten the visceral excitement of what it means to be a fully spiritual and sexual being. Too busy with their profession, family or a host of other distractions, they lose their passion and then wonder why life falls flat. One woman in my spirituality group described it like this: "I have forgotten what it means to be a sexual being. I've used my overabundance of activity, my very rewarding career, my wonderful kids. . . . I've used it all as reasons for not being more sensual and sexual. Not to

46

be a sexual being, and to tune out when the subject of sex is brought up, makes me feel numb. By denying my sexuality I feel like I am slapping God in the face. So now I am exploring what it takes to awaken my feelings again."

Where do you start? Well, let's look at where Leah may have started—in the privacy of her own tent, where she communed with Asherah, and according to the Zohar, the Shekinah, the feminine aspect of the Hebrew God.[28] She could have decorated her space with symbols that were meaningful to her from both traditions. In the Bahir, the ancient kabbalistic text, it says that "the seed of the date has a split like a woman. . . . paralleling it is the power of the moon."[29] She may have placed these seeds upon her personal altar as a powerful reminder of her womanhood.

You can begin creating your own similar sacred space by finding somewhere in your environment where you can close the door and turn off the phone. Choose a corner of your bedroom, or maybe the bathroom, and anoint and adorn this space in a manner that portrays who you are and reflects your beliefs. To further consecrate your space, create an altar and assemble fragrance, music, candles and other objects that empower your womanhood. Place the altar near a full-length mirror. If you have no room to call your own, like a woman I know, you can create your very own private space in a closet. Living in a crowded apartment, she rearranged the small clothes closet in a way that allowed room for her to sit on the floor, light a piece of incense, turn on a tiny scarf-covered lightbulb and proudly take in the walls, which were artfully covered with memorabilia and a large poster of a marble Buddha. Sitting in her sanctuary, I was inspired by the magic with which she transformed space and altered my sense of time.

Once you have prepared your environment, you may want to relax in a bubble bath or sensual shower, or take a few moments to meditate. When you are comfortably relaxed, look at yourself in the mirror. Your body is both a mirror and an expression of the Divine. Notice your image and body posture. How do you see yourself? Start with the face. What is your expression? Notice the obvious and subtle changes in the facial muscles as your expression changes. Become so familiar with your image that you can close your eyes and still see it reflected in the mirror.

Explore your body in the mirror by your altar, observe yourself fully. Become aware of your body and your attitude toward it. It is a complex system requiring the simplest maintenance, and the deepest appreciation. Notice its subtleties. Let your eyes caress the angles and curves of your figure as you move. If this embarrasses you, consider your body as it is described in the Song of Songs, a collection of poems of human love that can also speak of how precious our bodies are to God:

LEAH

The curves of your thighs are like jewels,
the work of a skilled craftsman.
Your navel is a rounded goblet
that never shall want for spiced wine.
Your belly is like a heap of wheat
set about the lilies.
Your two breasts are like two fawns,
twin fawns of a gazelle.
Your neck is like a tower of ivory.
Your eyes are pools in Heshbon,
beside the gate of the crowded city.
Your nose is like towering Lebanon
that looks toward Damascus.
You carry your head like Carmel . . .
How beautiful, how entrancing you are,
my loved one, daughter of delights!

Song of Songs 7:2–6

You too are a daughter of delights. So become familiar
with the form that carries you and houses your spirit. Close
your eyes and think about where you are most, and least,
comfortable in your body. Get a good sense of how you feel
being in your body. And then touch your pulse and feel

49

how God is breathing life into you with the same breath
that breathed life into Adam's soul. Become still enough to
hear the sound of God breathing into you. Imagine your
breath as the breath of God, inhaling and exhaling, con-
tracting and expanding through each pore, muscle, bone
and organ of your body. Once you are at home in your body,
you are at home with God. Just as the female aspect of God,
the Shekinah, dwelt within Leah, She also dwells within
you.

I know it is difficult for some people to feel or picture
God. For many it is easier to feel God in another rather than
in themselves. Some find it easier to imagine beings, guides
or angels, than to imagine God. And this is fine, because
God cannot be confined to any one thing but is all things, in
all places, at all times. And God comes to you in whatever
form is most comfortable. Every part of you is a part of God.
God is a way of thinking, speaking and acting that ex-
presses your sensual, sexual and spiritual nature. When I
feel God permeating my body it is the sensation of holiness
and purity. However, my image of God is not carved in
stone and can change as my life changes and evolves. Knowing that I walk with God adds light to a dreary day. Feeling
that I eat with God helps me have a greater appreciation for
the colors, textures and taste, as well as the intention with
which the food was created. Knowing that just as God's
voice speaks to my spirit, God also speaks to the spirits of

the people with whom I live, work and play enriches me. Experiencing God in all we think, say and do enhances our relationships and our encounters. It is with this way of thinking of God that we are able to make love to ourselves, to others and to our lives in general.

God does not only love you, but God is love in all of its forms. Therefore making love is sacred. And making love to another is just as holy as making love to life. Many people consult God when they need to make a decision, but when they make love to another, they want God to disappear, as though the lovemaking is un-Godly. As if God is OK from the neck up, but not from the neck or waist down. Rabbi Zalman Schachter-Shalomi calls this a part-time God living in a part-time body. Yet God, however you picture God to be, is a full-time God living in all parts of your body and life.

I found God, and She's in me.

Ntozake Shange[30]

When one woman in my group reported her experience with creating a sacred space and exploring her body, she said, "I didn't have a candle and couldn't find a match. So I just stood in front of the mirror and looked. I saw my nakedness. At first I started picking at the parts I'd like to change, then I said, 'No, no don't do that. Look at your goodness.' It felt a little weird until I allowed my eyes to look at the beauty of just being human." Another woman who had begun her experience having difficulty imaging God experienced an epiphany. She described it like this: "I thought to myself, 'I really have no idea who God is,' and as soon as I said that, God appeared and was here for me. I just let go trying to see what or who God is. And as soon as I released the expectation from my mind, God appeared. It was a sensation of feeling God all through my body. God was everywhere, and I felt so beautiful."

Finally, we learn from Leah how to utilize our everyday experiences as stepping stones to the Divine. She teaches us that it is possible to fully express and choreograph our thoughts, words, sensations and actions in a manner that aids God in sanctifying life. She inspires us to explore our bodies with openness and passion, and to discover the universe of potential within ourselves. We can love not because we are given it by another, but because we can stimulate it within ourselves. Leah's triumph reminds us that after the labor pains of our own rebirthing we can soar on the wings of God, held aloft by self-discovery.

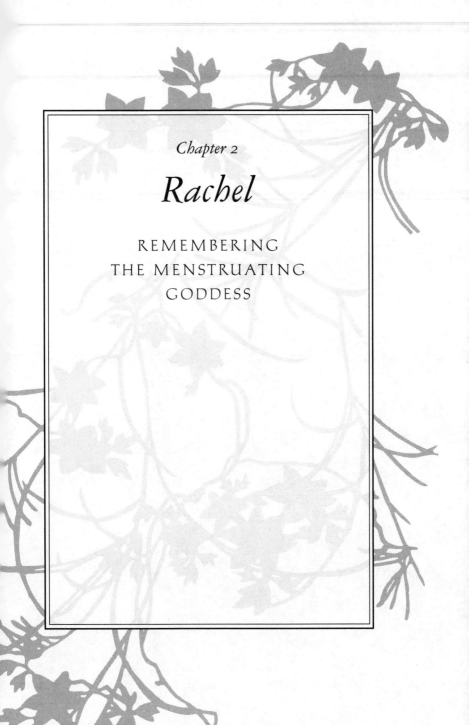

Chapter 2

Rachel

REMEMBERING THE MENSTRUATING GODDESS

*A*fter many years of living in his father-in-law's home, Jacob dreamed that God told him to return to the home of his father. He shared this dream with his wives, Rachel and Leah, and they both welcomed the opportunity to leave their father, Laban. After all, they had no ties to their domineering, intimidating father. They weren't even sure he would give them their due inheritance. So the sisters and their families prepared to leave. They waited until Laban was at a celebration of the shearing of his flocks and left in the wee hours of the morning. Before they left, Rachel went back into the house and took her family's treasured household gods.

It took three days before Laban realized his daughters and their families were gone, and that his prized gods were missing. He pursued them in the desert, and after seven days he reached their campsite and demanded the return of the deities. Jacob, stunned at the fact that someone could have stolen them, vowed to kill the thief, if found. Meanwhile, Laban searched everywhere to no avail. When he came to Rachel's tent, she apologized for not standing up as she was "in woman's way," meaning she had her period. But unbeknownst to her father she was hiding the gods in the pouch of the camel saddle on which she sat. Though unsuccessful in his search, Laban made amends to Jacob, erected an altar to God, celebrated through that night and, in the morning, blessed his family and returned to Haran. Rachel, Leah, Jacob, the hidden gods and their household continued on the road to Canaan.[1]

Now Rachel had taken the teraphim, put them in the saddle of the camel and sat upon them. And Laban searched the tent, but did not find them. And she said to her father, "Do not be angry that I cannot stand before you, for I am in the way of woman."

Genesis 31:34–35

RAGS AND blood. One brilliant red drop at a time, drawing patchwork images on the fabric of a woman's soul.

In the silence of a new dawn, Rachel prepared for her journey to independence. As the moon covered the rest of Laban's household with sleep, Rachel, Leah, Jacob and their children and servants were quietly and quickly packing the camels for the long journey from Laban's home in Padam-Aram to a new life with Jacob's father, Isaac, in distant Canaan.

Rachel felt that since her mother died, Laban had dominated their life long enough, and now she, Leah and Jacob were escaping in the dawn to follow their dreams. They would leave before Laban returned from the sheep-shearing ritual. This way they would avoid confrontation.

Just as you do when you pack for a long trip, Rachel looked around the home of her childhood one last time and asked herself, "What am I missing?" Her children, her husband, her sister and her sister's children, along with their household servants and Jacob's employees and all their possessions were ready and waiting outside in the caravan. She could hear the mules kick, the camels chew and the horses snort. The people were silent. Even the children held their breath. Amidst the frigid silence, Rachel stood still on the dirt floor in the courtyard of the house that held so many memories. It was here that she ran to tell her father about meeting Jacob that first time, at the well of living visons.[2] If she turned her head to the left and looked through the gate, she could see the well in the distance. As though it were happening now, at this moment, she recalled how Jacob rolled the stone from the well's mouth, watered her sheep, kissed her, cried out for joy, wept and then introduced himself. Ordinarily she would have been shocked by such behavior, but she knew the legend of the well and the supernal love that was conveyed in Jacob's kiss.[3] This was the well where the angel revealed to Hagar the future of her son, Ishmael;[4] where Rebekah was told of her marriage to Isaac;[5] Zipporah was told of her union to Moses;[6] Moses foresaw the vision of Zipporah;[7] and Jacob foresaw the vision of Rachel;[8] and since Rachel was a prophetess[9] who inhabited the spirit of Shekinah[10] and was herself an angel,[11] we can surmise that at this same well Rachel too was forewarned of Jacob's arrival.

Now as she stood on the threshold of a new journey she heard the whisper of her mother's voice. It seemed to resonate throughout the rooms, moving Rachel to the treasured box hidden on the uppermost shelf of Laban's room, next to his altar. Inside the box were the most treasured family possessions, the prized and cherished household gods—or teraphim—which now spoke to her through her mother's voice.[12] Everyone knew that the teraphim held the power over a person's prosperity. The goddess figurines not only guarded the family inheritance; they *were* the family inheritance, and as in other matrilineal traditions, these were given to the youngest daughter of the family.[13] With one hand Rachel held the teraphim and with the other hand she deftly replaced the emptied box on the topmost shelf, exactly where it had stood before. Then she slipped the teraphim in the pouch that hung over her stomach and rested on her crotch. With each step Rachel took toward the door, she was aware that she was finally walking away from her father's demeaning influence. She reached for the handle on the door, and as she opened it for the last time, she could hear the spirit of her mother's voice and the angelic chorus of the women of all time singing *halleluyah*. Though traditionally that word means "praise God," in the Zohar *halleluyah* means "praise her," referring to Rachel, whom it describes as the mother of the house.[14]

The moon gave way to the sun, and the sun turned its face to the moon, and the red and white of the desert days and nights intermingled. Three days passed and Laban sought answers to his family's sudden flight from him. He did what he had always done when he had more questions than answers, and reached for the high shelf to seek answers, solace and comfort from the teraphim. He took down the treasured box and was stunned to find the goddesses missing. This was not a good omen—with the disappearance of the teraphim, his whole fortune would be in jeopardy. What was he to do?

In fury, Laban gathered an army of men to hound Jacob, following his trail until they reached the caravan. Laban came flapping through the opening of Jacob's tent like a stormy wind. He demanded an explanation. Laban did not come to bully or banter, but he demanded an explanation. Jacob kept his cool. He had no idea that anyone had stolen the treasured goddesses, so he offered to help Laban not only find the thief but kill him as well.

Laban self-righteously blew in and out of the doors of each one's tent, searching for the teraphim, armed to kill.

When he reached Rachel's tent, he abruptly paused. What was it that froze him in his tracks? Was it the odor of blood, so different from his own? A blood that had the power over life rather than death. Was it the radiant light that glowed from his daughter Rachel's face as she sat proudly on the rags that held a painting of her soul? Little did he know that beneath the dripping red was the pouch that held the much-beloved goddesses. Perhaps it was the dreaded taboo surrounding menstruation that gave him pause? Whatever it was, it was foreign and frighteningly far from Laban's clenched fist of control. His domination and intimidation succumbed to the power of the mystery that dwelled in the blood of Rachel and the goddess beneath her womb.

As we journey with Rachel through the desert to her destiny, we discover the enduring connections between a woman's menstrual blood, the moon and the teraphim that Rachel claimed as hers. As Rachel's story unfolds, we can recognize how we've denied ourselves the bloodline of our heritage and how we can now, like Rachel, reclaim the healing powers of the teraphim through the natural cycles of our bodies.

the blood is the soul . . .

Deuteronomy 12:23

Menstrual blood. For centuries, for many cultures, it was a thing to be revered. In Greek and Indian mythology it is referred to as "miraculous wine," treasured for its magical powers. They tell mythic tales of drinking it, bathing in it and blessing it as a way to give and sustain life—even the lives of gods were dependent on the goddesses' menstrual blood.[15] It is also symbolized by the red thread used in the biblical tale of Rahab, an innkeeper hospitable to the Israelite spies, in Joshua 2. When it came time for the Israelites to overtake her Canaanite city, Rahab hung a red string from her inn as a symbol of life so the Israelites would keep her family alive and safeguard her home. To this day, many Sephardim[16] hang red strings above the cribs of newborn babies, in order to ward off evil spirits. In Song of Songs 2:4 the bride enters the "wine house" with her beloved, saying: "He has brought me to the winehouse, and spread his banner of love over me." And in Song of Songs 8:2 when the bride and beloved unite, she lets him drink from the red wine of her pomegranate, saying: "I will lead you into my mother's house, and she will teach me how to let you drink of the fragrant wine of my pomegranate." The wine implying female blood is also associated with the juice of a pomegranate, which, because of its many seeds, is symbolic of female genitals.[17]

The ancients believed the world began from the clotting of a goddess's menstrual blood at the time of the full moon;

this belief manifests itself in several creation accounts. According to Mesopotamian mythology, the goddess Mammetun made the first man out of earth and infused him with her life-giving blood, then taught women to form fertility charms from earth and cover them with menstrual blood.[18] The Bible tells of the creation of the first prototype human, Adam, made from *dam* and *adamah,* the Hebrew words meaning "blood" and "earth." In many traditions, sacred or taboo objects were marked with blood or red paint. Australian Aborigines would paint sacred stones, called *churingas,* with red ocher, symbolic of menstrual blood, and use them during religious rituals. The blood cloth of a menstruating woman symbolized the blood cloth of the menstruating goddess and was used for healing illness in India.[19] The Huichol Indians of America wrote their prayers with menstrual blood drawings.[20] In Greece red amulets, symbolic of the redeeming blood of Isis, would be buried with the dead to facilitate their journey into the next life.

Woman's menstrual blood, as symbolized in the "red carpet" or "red-sea of life," paved the way for the processions of queens, kings, brides and heroes.[21] Walking this path is akin to a newborn birthing its way through the birth canal. The Greeks, for instance, were born again in the River Styx, also known as "the bloodstream of the earth's vagina."[22] The biblical image of a similar river of life is the Red Sea through whose channels the Israelites were birthed from slavery into freedom. Following their passage through the Red Sea, the Israelites journeyed to Mount Sinai, which is also referred to by the Mesopotamians as the Mount of Sin, meaning the "mountain of the moon."[23]

And the seventh day was a Sabbath to God . . .
Exodus 16:29

Bless the Sabbath day and keep it holy.
Exodus 20:11

The most lasting menstrual tradition rests in the goddess Asherah. The Babylonians honored the fact that she, like her human counterparts, had menstrual cycles. They called menstruation *sabattu,* which is a derivative of the Babylonian word *sa-bat,* or "heart rest," the time when the moon is at its fullest and becomes still, neither waxing nor waning. The Asherah-worshiper believed the goddess menstruated at the time of the full moon. So each full moon, in honor of Asherah's menstruation, became a festival day of rest when the people ceased labor. Through time, they included the day of the new moon as well, and then the days of the quarter moon, until there was a rest day each week of

63

the month. *Sabattu* was the forerunner of the Sabbath as we know it now.[24] Just as menstruation is a time for rest and renewal, the root letters of the Hebrew word *teraphim* mean to heal, cure, restore and make whole. The Asherah teraphim themselves didn't heal or cure, but they were symbolic of a deeper feminine spirit in the universe that accomplished the same.

As I think of Rachel's legacy and the generations of ritual, worship and symbolism invested in the teraphim, I am able to more deeply appreciate the religious heirloom I inherited from my mother, which she inherited from hers: a pair of Sabbath candlesticks. Numerous stories are told of Jewish immigrants who had to leave one home or one country for another, and no matter how much or how little they could escape with, they always managed to take their mother's Sabbath candlesticks. I thought the Sabbath candlesticks were a symbol just for Jewish women, yet now I see that they take their place in the matriarchal lineage of Rachel's teraphim, the menstruating goddess and the tradition of Sabbath and can speak to all women.

It was the custom in Mesopotamia to carry the Asherah figurines whenever someone left their home for a new location. In 1 Kings we read that when King Asa ruled in Israel, his mother, Maachah, gave up her queendom in order to retain her Asherah images.[25] And when Gideon, in the Book of Judges, took ten men with him to cut down the

Asherah statues, the Israelites of Ofra were ready to kill him, and needless to say, he did not succeed.

Asherah figurines were found during all stages of the biblical period in all segments of Israelite society, yet there were few if any male figurines found in Israelite or indeed in any other homes of the Neolithic and early historic periods in the Near and Middle East. In fact, most pagan idols had breasts.[26] This is an indication of how prevalent the goddess worship was during that time. According to inscriptions found in northeast Sinai, the Hebrew God, Yahweh, and Asherah were worshiped simultaneously and may have been considered a divine couple.[27]

The voice of the angel of the well wasn't the only voice of the past that came to Rachel that morning. There was also the voice of Jacob, who indicated that his reason for returning to his homeland was to connect with his father's God, and said: "My Father's God has stood by me." (Genesis 31:16) Rachel understood the deeper meaning to this: It meant that the men and women of her time, as illustrated in her own family, were struggling with their allegiance to various male and female images of God. She heard her own voice as she responded, despite the fact that Laban treated her like a stranger, sold her into marriage and devoured her wealth,[28] saying: "Isn't there still a part of me in my father's house, an inheritance that is mine?"[29]

The need for a feminine image of God existed throughout Jewish history and comes to us today in the form of the Shekinah, who is considered synonymous with the moon[30] and the female partner of Yahweh.

There are several threads that link Rachel's destiny with the rightful ownership and protection of the teraphim. Like her sister Leah, and Abraham's wife, Sarah, before them, Rachel came from a background in which women named their own children, sent their sons to their own families of origin (rather than their husband's) to seek wives and retained their own traditions of goddess worship. Scholars differ over who retained rights to the inheritance during that time period. It appears that the local custom of the ancient Near and Middle East was that fathers gave inheritance rights to their sons. However, the traditions of other matrilineal societies, such as the Khasis and Garos of Southeast Asia, show the inheritance rights being given from the mothers to their youngest daughters. In both these societies, as in the time of the biblical matriarchs, the sons married into the families of their mother's relatives.[31]

The Zohar, the kabbalistic Book of Splendor, describes the Shekinah as an angel that sometimes appears in the form of a human messenger. It goes on to say that Rachel was really the Shekinah, but was perceived by Jacob in the human form of Rachel.[32] We can see Rachel as an angel sent with a message to safeguard and honor woman's traditions, who in order to relay that message as a legacy through time, reclaimed what was divinely hers by right. There is a tradition within Judaism called *Birkat Halevanah,* "blessing the moon," which consists of a prayer of gratitude recited on the eve of each new moon, or shortly thereafter. The Talmud says, "One who blesses the moon in the proper time is like one who is received by the Shekinah." (Sanhedrin 42a) Once again, the Shekinah, this time as Rachel, and the moon are linked with each other. From this we learn that there is a wholly other part to blessing the moon and that is the part that needs to come from the greater story of the power of woman's blood and the honoring of woman's menstrual cycle, or what we could call woman's moontime.

After reading about the connections of the moon with a woman's moontime and its sacredness in ancient tradition, you may be asking yourself: Why wasn't I taught any of this? So let me remind you how important stories are— whether they are mythical, biblical or personal. When you change the story, you can change the whole culture. This is what the patriarchal era did in history, and women have the power now to correct it. But first let me tell you how it happened. It didn't happen overnight. It occurred over several thousand years as northern warrior tribes invaded the Near and Middle Eastern regions and brought with them male deities to whom the goddesses of the regions they conquered were ultimately forced to submit.[33] At first the northern invaders and the patriarchal leaders of the regions integrated the two dieties, as the descendents of Rachel and Jacob integrated the Hebrew god, Yahweh, with the goddess Asherah.[34] This act wasn't unusual for them or Rachel and Jacob because they lived in a society where allegiance was pledged to numerous gods simultaneously. The difficulty came when the gods competed for allegiance, as Jacob experienced in his dream that led him back to the God of his father.

Then the stories changed from goddess-oriented tales honoring a woman's body to god-oriented tales of dishonoring woman and covering up the mysteries of her body. Eventually the male deities became all-powerful and the goddesses were reduced to symbols of darkness and evil.

In the Babylonian myth of Marduk, who brutally murdered the goddess Tiamat in order to secure his position as supreme diety, so the story goes, he split Tiamat in two and used her body parts to separate heaven from earth.[35] These new stories of patriarchy hailed the male god and initiated dualistic thinking, an either/or mentality in which everything existed in opposition rather than in harmony with each other. Similar stories surfaced in Sumeria, where the goddesses became the consorts to the gods, who weakened them. And in one Sumerian legend even the goddess of the underworld is dragged from her throne by her hair and forced not only to marry her assailant but to give him the all-powerful Tablets of Destiny.[36]

In Jewish legends this depreciation of women was a bit more subtle but just as devastating. One Jewish legend tells the story of how the female-moon and the male-sun were created as two great lights, equal in size and importance. But because of jealousy between them, God decided to make the moon smaller, especially since the moon encroached on the sun on the days when the moon is visible even while the sun is out. After which, God felt sorry for the moon and appeased it by accompanying it with stars.[37]

These are simplistic tales, yet they moved deep into the psyche of the people, pushing the goddess into centuries of oblivion. Both men and women have forgotten the stories of her benevolent powers, and the blood of a menstruating woman is foreign and puzzling to a man's experience. What do you mean shedding blood without pain? How can this blood of woman be life giving, when all the blood men shed was death oriented?[38] Some even thought that the menstrual blood came from too much sex!

What drove patriarchy to change the story? The patriarchy recognized that there was a power to a menstruating woman, but they didn't understand what that power was and assumed it was dangerous and demonic. When we fear what we cannot understand, we place boundaries around it, like caging a wild animal because we are afraid of the animal. Then we tell horror stories about the animal. We say that if you touch it you will be stained or deformed for life, its babies are demons and its eyes can throw curses, its sounds can destroy cities. The same thing happened to woman. She became the isolated, caged animal, confined during her menstrual period, often to dark rooms for anywhere from two weeks to one year, depending on the country and culture. She could not be touched, or seen, or heard during the time of her blood flow.

The disempowering stories that came about from a fear of woman's potency during her period became the basis for increasing forms of male-dominated practices in religion. Whether in the primitive societies of Africa, Australia or the Americas, or among the civilized societies of Europe, foreboding laws were written that forbid men even the slightest association with a menstruating woman.[39] These laws warned that if a man came in touch with a menstruating woman he could lose his wisdom, energy, vitality, strength or sight. In the Talmud, the rabbis warned that if a menstruating woman walked between two men, one of them would surely die.[40] As one friend jokingly puts it, "The taboos were against everything a woman could or could not do. Men couldn't touch her body, her dishes or eat from her plate. But not once did they say she couldn't cook!"

Despite the discrediting propaganda and disempowering taboos, women today are empowering themselves and rewriting the story of how their lives need to be. We are beginning to reconnect with our own natural body rhythms, with the ebbs and flows of our life-giving blood and with the need to not only release our blood, but release centuries of pent-up emotions as well. We are no longer caged animals imprisoned by the falsifications of old paradigms. The goddess is back. The teraphim that Rachel hid proudly are now safely seated in the niches of women's altars, like that of my friend whom I described in chapter 1. They are no longer just figurines, they are the figurative ways in which we can see, hear and sense ourselves to be. They are a new kind of inheritance that connects today's menstruating woman with yesterday's goddess and tomorrow's daughter.

The legacy of the teraphim is also showing up in our art. Women's menstrual blood has been given a place of honor in Judy Chicago's work. She started with the lithograph of a bloody tampon, which she called *Red Flag*. Then she went on to design, with others, a Womanhouse, an actual house reconstructed by women about women. In the house was a Menstruation Bathroom in which all the menstrual paraphernalia that most of us hide in trash cans, roll up in napkins, disguise with deodorizers and wash off toilet seats, Chicago put out in the open as prized, precious trophies. (Maybe that's why "trophy" sounds a bit like teraphim?) When I saw this bathroom I was at first shocked, for I too used to roll my bloody tampon in oodles of toilet paper (so no one should see the blood), even though I was only putting it in the garbage can one foot away. But I felt proud too, because the work of art was welcoming menstruating women out of the closet and into life, no longer hidden.

Once we know the legacy of the teraphim, we have a more positive appreciation for the magic of menstruation and the ritual honoring of woman's blood. We can no longer say once upon a time woman's blood was sacred, but now it's smelly, ugly and foul. When we get our periods, we can no longer look at ourselves and think we are anything less than holy and whole. When we get full, we need to empty and take a "heart rest" or sabbath day. As one woman in my group said, "PMS means: pause, meditate and take a sabbath." We can no longer succumb to the fear of fitting into a time frame that is unnatural to the rhythm of a woman's sacred body. We no longer need to get depressed because we are being pushed by a clock instead of our bodies. A woman's body doesn't always work best from nine to five. That doesn't mean she is less productive; rather, she is more creative when she is in tune with her own inner rhythm. Several women I know who are in corporate settings are opting to take work home during the day, rather than sit in an office. They feel that at home, in their own leisure setting, with flexible hours, they get more accomplished than in the structured time frame of the office. When we know our story of the matriarchal past, we no longer need to get *depressed* but can move to fully *express* ourselves.

Wearing red to ward off negativity is still popular today. Some women wear red dresses or suits to feel powerful or to make a statement of strength. The same can be accomplished with red accessories, lipstick—even though many women may have no idea that wearing red as a confidence booster comes from the power of their own menstrual blood. One woman I know wears red nail polish when she feels the need for extra protection from outside influences or negative energy.

How do we maintain our new knowledge and our renewed image of ourselves? By continuing to tell our own empowering stories. And if you find your story is not empowering, then change it! When you change your story, you change your attitude, and you change your life. One night as we were discussing our experiences with menstruation in my women's group, one woman spoke of her experience and how she changed the story for her daughter. She said, "I was the first in my class to get my period. I came home with blood on my pants, and I was so scared. I didn't understand what was happening. My mom got real upset and sent my dad out to get sanitary napkins. He was embarrassed, and I got the message from the beginning that this was something upsetting and embarrassing. But when it came time for my daughter to get her period, I turned it into a celebration. First, I spoke to her way ahead of time and described it as a thrilling experience. Then in her first cycle, when her blood began to flow, I gave her an heirloom piece of jewelry that my grandmother gave to my mother and she gave to me. In this way I was letting my daughter know that now she was part of a sacred blood legacy."

Many other women that evening bemoaned the fact that they did not know about the legacy of the menstruating goddess. Had they been educated about their own bodies and its mysteries from ancient times on, they would have felt greater self-esteem and given more support to their daughters. They agreed that we need to put menstruation in a whole new context. We need to help our daughters create rituals for themselves in ways that honor their bodies while respecting their privacy. This could be done by educating the people in our families, having a party or dinner and letting our daughter feel like a celebrated goddess, or creating a mystery initiation for women only, or perhaps letting her stay home from school that day for a "heart rest." There have been a number of moontime rituals written up in magazines and books, and I think we need to be able to use them not only for the newly initiated, but for older women who have a need to relive and reempower that part of their lives. Rituals help us move beyond anger over the past and bring us to who we are now, vehicles for the Divine.

A friend of mine once relayed this vision she had when she practiced her own ritual—meditating on the Chariot of Light. Kabbalists meditate on a metaphoric "Chariot of Light" as a vehicle for connecting to God. One day, while she had her period, my friend felt her uterus become the chariot, described by the kabbalists as a light-permeable vehicle that takes you from one state of consciousness or nature to another. In the same way, she imagined that the lining of her uterine wall was shedding excess tissue in order to move her from one state of nature to another. She said, "The chariot is called *merkavah* in Hebrew, which comes from the word that means 'to ride.' When the Bible says that God 'rides,' it means that God leaves the natural state of being invisible and rides to the state of being 'seen' by the visionaries. The same with my menstrual blood. It travels from the hidden spaces, unseen by the naked eye, to the revealed, seen places outside of my body. When I meditated on the Chariot of Light, not only did I become the chariot, but my uterus became the chariot within the chariot, the light within the light." Listening to her story I was reminded of a passage I recalled while reading Aryeh Kaplan's book *Meditation and Kabbalah,* in which he quotes Maimonides' description of how one feels in meditative ecstasy. "This blood within you will begin to vibrate because

75

of the living permutation that loosens it. Your entire body will then begin to tremble, and all your limbs will be seized with shuddering. . . . you will feel as if an additional spirit is within you, arousing you and strengthening you, passing through your entire body and giving you pleasure. It will seem as though you have been anointed. . . ."[41]

May the women that God brings to you be like Rachel and Leah . . .

Ruth 4:11

The monthly cycle of blood was Rachel's rite of passage into woman's power and independence. Now it is ours. Along with our own stories, we need to continue to tell the story of who Rachel really was—an angel sent by the Shekinah, at the beginning of the patriarchal period, to safeguard the legacy of the menstruating goddess. She knew the power of woman's miraculous wine and would not stand for Laban's intimidation or domination. From her we can take courage not to deny the godliness of any part of our own bodies, nor disenfranchise ourselves from any aspect of life, for she wove a fabric of womanhood that still embraces us, centuries later, in her death. Rachel, who died on the way to her husband's home of Canaan, was buried in Bethlehem, and her tomb is a celebrated landmark, from biblical times until now, for all who enter transitional journeys. When the prophet Samuel anointed Saul for holy service to God, he instructed him to go to the tomb of Rachel as the first stop on his journey.[42] As she died on the way from one place to the next, she guides one in honoring the natural cycles of change. We can look to Rachel as an angel spreading her wings, like the teraphim, bestowing blessings upon us for health and prosperity as we withstand the ebb and flow of our lives.[43]

In the Book of Jeremiah, the prophet portrays Rachel weeping for her children—Israel—as she refuses to be comforted until they return from the land of their enemy. But I think Rachel is weeping for her daughters and granddaughters because they are not yet in their full empowerment. She understands that we are just now beginning to return from the estrangement of our bodies and the debilitation of our spirits. Yet, if we read the prophet's words in a different light, each drop of blood that flows from the spirit of woman will bring hope for a renewed life:

God says:
There is a voice in Ramah
Lamentation and bitter weeping,
Rachel weeping for her children;
She refuses to be comforted for her children . . .
So says God:

77

Refrain your voice from weeping
And your eyes from tears
For your work will be rewarded,
Says God;
And they will come back
from the land of the enemy.

There is hope for your future
says God;
And your children will return to
their own border.

Jeremiah 31:14–16

Chapter 3

Eve

UNITING WITH
THE DIVINE

*I*n the beginning of time, God created Adam in the image of God, both male and female in one body. God placed Adam in the Garden of Eden to till the land, eat of its fruit and name all the species of creation. Then one day God saw that Adam, though surrounded by every type of animal and plant, was alone. And God said, "Adam needs a proper and fitting partner." So God put Adam into a deep dreamlike state and fashioned Eve from the rib of Adam.

Eve and Adam were allowed to eat of all the fruits of the garden, but were forewarned that on the day that they would eat from the Tree of Knowledge, they would die. Now one day Eve was playing in the garden when the wise serpent inspired her to eat of the forbidden fruit of the Tree of Knowledge. Eve ate fruit from the Tree and then gave Adam a bite. Their eyes were opened to each other's nakedness, and from that time on Adam and Eve saw each other differently. God sent them from the garden into a whole new world where they knew each other as husband and wife and gave birth to the next generation.[1]

God created them male and female, and on the day when God created them, God blessed them and called their name Adam.

Genesis 5:2

SO THEY didn't start off being the perfect couple by human standards. Admittedly, it must have been awkward for them. On the day they were created they were not two distinct people. They shared a name and they shared a body. She and he were a he-she, two genders perfectly sculpted and joined at the hip.[2] For God this arrangement may have been perfect. But for the androgynous humanoid called Adam, it was wearisome and problematic.[3] Wherever he went, she went too, neither sure of their direction or footing, hobbling on four legs through what some have called paradise. Yet to Adam, the Garden of Eden was less like paradise and more like helpless childhood—constantly being cared for, with minimal opportunities for companionship.

Just imagine. They, Adam, called everything else in the garden—the birds, bees, flowers, and all creeping, crawling creatures—by name. But not once could the he and she of Adam really see, touch or speak face to face as two equals. They were similar to some couples today, who are attached to each other yet spend all their time penciling the other in and catering to everyone else's needs until they are unable to see each other as individuals, much less as friends, and least of all as lovers.

Soon Adam heard God's voice speak of their discomfort, saying, "Adam does not have a partner that fits." (Genesis

2:21–24) "Fits" is a gentle term God used to suggest that Adam needed someone who was spiritually and sexually functioning. Everyone needs a partner that fits, but not everyone is lucky enough to know that their true partner is right under their nose, attached to their hip. But they may discover that their true partner mirrors the he or she within themselves.

How did the androgynous Adam get a partner? Adam fell asleep and let God take over,[4] separating the she and he into two distinct entities: the first real man and the first real woman. So as not to add to their confusion, the woman let the man retain the name Adam. In this way, whenever the animals in the garden called Adam, he answered. But what did she answer to? She had to learn how to move into a new identity: Woman. Woman needed time before she could obtain a name that suited her essence. She needed to first discover who she was apart from Adam and know herself as an expression of the Creator.

Woman was so sensationally beautiful[5] that she became the object of everyone's indulgent attention. At first she thought all she had to do was sit and look pretty, because everything else was done for her by Adam and the creatures in the garden. She forgot that she was able to do things on her own; she forgot how to think for herself and how to make her own decisions. Eventually, the pampering made her lazy and bored. Then Woman befriended a serpent—a new creature in the garden, one that she hadn't noticed before.[6]

The serpent inspired Woman to venture through and revel in the garden. Day by day, Woman's true wise spirit emerged. While Adam was busy with his chores, she swam in the rivers, floated in the ponds and frolicked with the wildlife. Each time Woman gazed out at the garden she noticed new landscapes of splendor. She heard God's voice in the gentle winds and felt God's embrace in the small creatures and rustling trees.

One day as she meandered through the garden, God caused a mist to rise in front of her. In the warm veil of moisture, she heard the echoing voice of God forewarn her that when she would eat the fruit of the Tree of Knowledge that grew in the middle of the garden, she would die a certain death. Woman could not make her way forward until the mist subsided, yet she could see the serpent crossing her path. When Woman disclosed God's warning to the serpent, the serpent explained that we all at some point need to gain independence by finding the truth of who we are. Woman understood that if she ate the fruit of knowledge, she would fully understand her own sexuality and divinity. She would no longer be just a plain girl but would become a goddess. The serpent told her that dying meant dying to the old, and that she would no longer be satisfied remaining sequestered in Eden. If Woman ate the fruit, she had to be prepared to own her divinity and create her own place in the world outside of Eden.

With the sweat of anxiety beaded on her forehead, and the thumping of her heart echoing through to her finger-tips, the first woman reached for the fruit of the forbidden Tree of Knowledge. She smelled its fragrance, then gin-gerly bit into its skin. As she sucked the juice from its peel she felt a sudden tug at her heart. Her eyes opened to a rev-elation of her vulnerability, her strength and her God-like presence. At once, she perceived how to love more fully, how to live more divinely with all parts of herself and with Adam. She looked across the field to where Adam was till-ing the earth and saw the spirit within him. Even from that distance she could still sense the presence of God dwelling within both of them.

Like most women today, Woman wanted her partner, Adam, to share in this divine experience. She greeted Adam in his field and offered him a bite of the fruit, encouraging him to grow along with her by eating the fruit of knowl-edge. He bit into it, and the moment the nectar of the fruit of knowledge flowed through Adam, his awareness deep-ened, and he saw Woman as he had never seen her before—intelligent, creative, powerful and lifegiving. From deep within his soul a voice whispered that he should call his beloved by this name: Eve.[7]

Woman liked the name Eve (meaning "mother of all life," in Hebrew); it fit who she was. Psalm 19 may imply Eve's place in the matriarchal moon culture. Psalm 19:3 describes the heavens as revealing knowledge of "night to night." In Hebrew, the words for "reveals knowledge" are *yekhawweh daat;* these are traditionally translated as "[God] reveals knowledge." *Daat* refers to an intimate knowing. But the root letters of *yekhawweh (chof, vet, hey)* also spell *Khawwah,* which is Eve's name in Hebrew. Therefore, Eve was an instrument through which God revealed the mysteries of the moon.

Khawwah may be an Hebraicized form of Heba, Hebat, Khebat or Kheba, who was the wife of the Hittite storm god worshiped in Jerusalem.[8] In Phoenicia the goddess Astarte was called Eve, in Assyria, Nin-Eveh or "Holy Lady Eve," and in Babylonia she was called the "Goddess of the Tree of Life."[9] Furthermore the Arabic words for Eve, serpent and life were all derived from the same root word, which is similar to *Khawwah.*[10] Eve was the embodiment of both God and Life, and the archetypal image of *hieros gamos,* the sacred marriage.

But who was this serpent? Was it an entity that came to remind Woman of her true potential beyond her appearance? Many biblical translators have described the serpent as cunning and crafty, as though the serpent was less than virtuous. However, the same Hebrew word for cunning, *arum,* can mean "wise, prudent or cautious." Sacred serpents roamed freely throughout goddess temples in the Neolithic period. Sumerian theology saw the serpent as a god in his own right, called "Lord of the Tree of Truth,"[11] and his female counterpart was called the "Great Mother Serpent of the Heaven." In Egypt the serpent not only was a goddess but became the hieroglyphic symbol for that word,[12] and in Babylonia the goddess was attended by a serpent who watched over the fruit of immortality. The Australian serpent Puana, also a representation of eternal life, created the world by shedding its skin, beginning in the earth beneath the waters and then spraying the heavens with stars in its serpentine path upward.[13]

Perhaps the serpent in the Bible was God in disguise. According to anthropologist and biblical scholar Dr. Raphael Patai, the Hebrew God had at one time been identified with a serpent god.[14] Jewish medallions of the first and second centuries B.C.E. depicted such a god. According to historian Joseph Campbell, the seraphim (the Hebrew name given to the guardian angels of God) were originally serpent spirits.[15] The sacred serpent wove its way through the Israelite culture—for example, during the Israelite exodus from Egypt, the name of the first man who walked into the Red Sea as the waters were rising above his head, before the sea split and dry land appeared, was Nakhshon, whose name meant serpent.[16] This is more than a coincidence, for the serpent was not only believed to rule over the water,[17] but as well, symbolized leaving the past behind in its shedding of skin. When Nakhshon entered the sea he was leading the Israelites from the shackles of slavery and into a new land of freedom.

This background helps us to see that God may have purposefully placed the serpent in Woman's path in order to inspire Eve to unite with God through eating the fruit of knowledge so she could shed her old passive ways. Retranslating this pivotal story gives modern women a frame of reference from which we can grow. It shows us that we can shed old skins and be confident of slipping into new roles, even if it means leaving one kind of Eden and traveling to a new form of paradise. For some women this could mean a change of job, location, or—most importantly—an attitude change. This is unlike the Melanesian tale that tells of an old woman who went to the stream to cast away her old skin and became young again. When she returned home, her child screamed and wailed and refused to recognize her. So in a frustrated rage—in order to keep peace in her family—she went back to the river, retrieved her old skin and, once again, returned home as an old hag. From that time on, the people of Melanesia, Papua and Celebes claimed, humans ceased to live forever and began to die.[18] In contrast, Eve is telling us to shed our old skins and keep them off even if we have to change our environment—to not be afraid to outgrow a job, a location or a way of being. She shows us that as we move forward in our lives, our loved ones will also be motivated to grow. Rather than being held back by Adam, Eve offered him the fruit of knowledge, and he also grew.

The first woman's decision to initiate her own enlightenment brought fear to generations to follow. What they thought may have been the first woman's fall can be read as the step that led her and all women to a sacred marriage with the Divine, much like the myth of Psyche ascending the mountain to marry Death. The interpreters of the Bible, the religious scholars, leaders and teachers, squelched the power of the first woman, falsely blaming her for bringing death into the world. They limited the translation of the Hebrew words *mot tamut* in Genesis 2:17 to mean "you will certainly die" when it could also mean "you will die a certain kind of death," thus indicating that God's warning to Woman was: "On that day when you eat from it [the Tree], *you will certainly die,*" rather than "On that day when you will eat from it [the Tree], *you will die a certain kind of death.*"

It may not be easy to eat the fruit of knowledge, when traditional religions still advise against it. But it may also prove daunting because that knowledge contains insights into your own sexuality that you may not be ready to confront. Not all women are ready to become goddesses in their own right. The first woman perhaps had her own doubts: Was she good enough to be a goddess? Would the knowledge of good and bad change her positive attitude? Could she handle the power of her sexuality? Would Adam still love her? Would the male God be her friend if she owned her divinity? We may have similar concerns, but we do not need to worry. When a woman owns her divinity, she becomes more comfortable with her figure and sees it as another image of who God is on earth, and accepts abundance and pleasure as her rightful claim. This brings to mind the expression coined by a friend of mine: "good guilt." When anyone says to her they feel guilty for being so blessed when others are suffering, or for having so much good when there is so much bad, she says, "Great. That's a good guilt. Keep it up and the world will change." This doesn't mean you stop giving and sharing with those less fortunate. It only means you stop feeling you need to forfeit your own joy on account of another's deprivation. Instead, choose to focus on the gift you have been given, on the positive, and things will change.

For Eve and Adam saw God not as a punishing authority figure handing down verdicts, but as a source of female and male energy that touched all of life, one that blessed them, clothed them[19] and sent them into the new world to increase. Eve and Adam's godliness made them compassionate companions for each other and gave them the strength to cope with the challenges that would surface along their path. They walked out of the gates of Eden hand in hand and soul in soul.

Eve and Adam can guide us in a most sacred way of loving each other and uniting with God. Our journey toward creating a meaningful sacred union starts with Adam *knowing* Eve. As mentioned before, in Hebrew, *daat,* the word "to know," implies an intimate knowledge of one's self and another, as intimate as lovemaking. In Judaism knowledge is very much associated with sex. When the Bible states that "Adam *knew* Eve" (Genesis 4:1) it means they made love and birthed new life. When a woman feels "known" and the divinity within her is acknowledged, she will birth new worlds of experiences for herself and for those whose lives she touches.

What does it mean to be known or to know another? Do you ever feel truly known? And by whom? To know someone transcends a biological act; it is the sacred union of two lives, two souls and two destinies. When you make love to another, the God that is within you unites with the God that is within your partner.

I just a met a woman who is unhappy in her marriage and considering divorce. When I asked her, "What is the most painful part of your relationship with your husband?" she answered, "He doesn't honor my God." Knowing they are of the same religion, I asked her to explain what that meant to her. She said, "When we are together there is no reverence or awe; he doesn't respect my spiritual connection to God. When we make love he feels good, but that's about it. I don't feel the music. It's like sounds without melody, or shapes without color. There's no soul interaction, and the spirit in me feels like it's dying. I can't let my spirit die." This need for sharing is reiterated in Genesis 25:21, which describes Isaac's and Rebekah's dilemma. He was anxious that she become pregnant, so he "*entreated* the Lord for his wife, because she was barren."[20] The Hebrew word *vayehtar,* translated as "entreated," could also mean "to enrich." Perhaps Isaac needed to enrich his own relationship with God before he could truly "know" Rebekah and birth new life.

To know or be known intimately, start, like Eve, with discovering where the divine resides inside you. Once you are comfortable exploring your body and seeing it as a miracle of creation, you will have greater confidence to share the gift of who you are with your partner. One evening in my women's group I posed the question: "How does it feel to include God in your lovemaking?" At first there were some questions as to who God is. And to most of the women, God was not a man with a long gray beard hovering over their beds, looking down on them through a hidden camera. God was an energy, a light, a loving ethereal presence that let them know they were special. Then one woman in the group said, "When I feel God inside of me there is no judgment. I don't think whether I'm doing it right or wrong—I only feel the expression of love." Another woman added, "I feel free and joyous, like all I want to do is love and give and not worry about receiving or performance." While another remarked, "If you could describe how truth feels, that's how I feel when God is in me. I feel so true. And when I don't feel God in my lovemaking, I'm not totally present. I'm thinking about what I have to do next. But being with God means being in the moment."

For many of the women, including God in their lovemaking had to do with communication; it heightened their ability to listen as well as their need to be heard. They agreed that compassionate listening and loving words can be as satisfying as a caress. For some women, just the touch of a hand, an embrace or catching a glimpse of another's soul in conversation are ways to know and be known.

No other love is like the ecstasy of the moment when spirit cleaves to spirit in a kiss.

Zohar 2: 146a

Another woman, whose husband had cancer, described how her marriage was transformed by the effect of his radiation therapy. His body was so painfully sensitive that she could not even touch him. She described how, for a period of eighteen months, she would lie next to him at night and not touch him, except for a kiss gently planted on his lips. All her love went into that most delicate kiss. Through that kiss they were known to each other.

The twentieth-century mystic Abraham Joshua Heschel said that ninety percent of the time the knowledge of *daat* is emotional. We women, who largely relate to each other through telling our stories and validating each other's feelings, can certainly vouch for that statement. What we give to each other as women, we yearn to be able to share with the men in our lives. To have true intercourse with a man, a woman needs to first feel safe sharing true and intimate feelings between herself and her partner. Men could save their energy, and probably their money too, if only they would listen to what women really want. And what we need is a two-way conversation that's real.

We need genuine conversation. The kind that is as explosive and satisfying as an orgasm. Let me explain. By an orgasmic relationship I mean one that is constantly and steadily exciting in all areas, not just in the bedroom. I once asked a middle-aged, professional American woman I know, "What would an orgasmic relationship feel like to you?" She described her relationship with a young African sales agent she was dating. She did not describe his physique or performance when she thought of their relationship as being orgasmic. Instead, she exclaimed, "It's the conversations we have. The conversations are so authentic, they are orgasmic." I would venture to say that seated in every pew and lying under every quilt you will find a woman yearning for similar talk. What we learn from the Bible and the story of Eve and Adam is that companionship comes before procreation as a primary incentive for sexual union. God first blesses Adam with a partner so he-she will not be alone; *then* God blesses them to "be fruitful and multiply." (Genesis 1:27, 28 and Genesis 2:18, 22)

Sex is not just procreation or biological intercourse, it is how we intercourse with life itself. Sex is the means by which we come to be and the intimacy with which we know life. Sex is not just an aspect of reality. It *is* our reality. Sex is how we connect to all things, inside and out; emotional and physical; rational and nonrational.[21] Orgasmic living goes beyond sexual techniques and skills; it means being fully open to the sensations and feelings of the moment, like crying in the movies, or screaming on a roller-coaster ride or making love without inhibition. It is no accident that the garden in the Bible was called Eden, for in Hebrew *eden* means "pleasures or delights." As one woman in my group put it, "Life is a wondrous journey, and as I become more conscious, everything holds possibilities for becoming an orgasmic experience." To a jet-setting, politically active woman I know, orgasm is in the laughter. "You can say the same thing to two different people and one remains masked in a stoneface while the other unselfconsciously guffaws. The orgasm is in the guffaws," she said to me with a broad smile on her face.

Can you imagine what it would be like if before you entered into union with another, you would come face to face with your partner, like Eve with Adam? What would happen if you spent time dropping the mask that you show to the rest of the world and entered the safe sanctuary of a loving partner? I know an exquisite single woman who wears a wig to cover her thinning hair. When she was describing some of her romantic escapades, I inquired, "Do you remove your wig during sex?" She answered, "I only get sexual with a man with whom I'm willing to be intimate. Then I want him to know all of me, as I him. And when I remove my wig and makeup, I am taking off the outer covering and showing him the most intimate parts of who I am. God is in the bare nakedness, where nothing is hidden. That to me is sacred sex."

In a Jewish wedding ceremony, before the bride and groom walk down the aisle, there is a ritual performed called *kabbalat panim,* or "receiving the faces," in which the groom lifts the veil of the bride, they greet each other, and then they replace the veil over her face. This occurs during the signing of the wedding contract and before consummating a marriage. We find echoes of this ritual in ancient

Sumerian mythology, where the primordial mother goddess who governed the fruitful garden was said to have hidden behind the veil of the young bride.[22] This ritual comes from the biblical story of Jacob and Leah. The rabbis said that because Jacob could not see through his bride's veil, he did not know that he was marrying Leah instead of his true betrothed, Rachel. In Kabbalah, the veil is both a protective shield and symbolic of the illusions we give ourselves, like the masks we wear that cover our true feelings. When the bride replaces her veil during the ceremony, she is protecting the intimacy of the union.

When I am the officiating rabbi at a wedding, I explain to the bride and groom that the *kabbalat panim* ritual, often done in a private room, is an opportunity for them to remove their masks and come face to face with each other. Before the wedding ceremony is about to begin, I ask the select witnesses to congregate in the room and to create a safe space for the bride and groom by closing their eyes and giving the wedding couple a moment of privacy. I then instruct the wedding couple to open their eyes to each other and imagine seeing deep within each other's soul. I reiterate that this is a time for them to put aside the masks they show the world and to unveil the true spirit of the one they are about to wed. This is a time to recognize the face of God within each other. To be known by each other as intimately as God is known within them. Then they are ready to unite not only their bodies in marriage, but their godliness as well. When they feel complete in the ritual, they each sign the wedding contract and declare before the witnesses that they will safely hold and help nurture the face of God in each other. This is a very moving moment of being *known*—for the couple, as well as for each of us in the room.

When Eve wanted sexual intimacy with Adam, it was because she wanted to share with him her godly essence. And he likewise with her. Yet they did more than share orgasms. They shared an ecstasy capable of spreading enormous healing energy. Similarly, when you share your orgasm with the one you love, you have the same capability of breaking through the inhibitions that have heretofore blocked your growth. The I-Ching says that the mystical power of loving sexual ecstasy is so potent it can give life to all things. Physical pleasure, according to the Baal Shem Tov, is the gateway to spiritual fulfillment, and the Zohar says that when there is love during intercourse, the physical pleasure becomes spiritual pleasure.[23] It's the same with joy. It will increase if you give your own joy to those around you. This is why the rabbis say that if you need a healing prayer, ask a bride who is about to be married to pray for you. Prayers said with ecstasy accelerate healing.

EVE

*Like a woman who receives a man, the upper and lower
waters pour into each other and produce a seed.*

Zohar 1:29b

The Zohar, the kabbalistic Book of Splendor, is replete
with erotic imagery of sexual union, teaching us that the
idea of knowing is metaphysical as well as emotional and
sexual. The Zohar states that, just as the King (Father-
God) needs the Shekinah (Mother-God), a man needs a
woman. It describes the union of heaven and earth as one
would describe the sexual union of male and female. Man
represents wisdom, woman represents understanding, and
the body is symbolic of the Holy of Holies, the innermost
chamber of the Temple sanctuary, which holds the spirit of
God. Therefore, in a loving union, wisdom unites with understanding in the Holy of Holies, and the result is a trans-
formative power that can shatter negativity in the world
and return balance to the universe. The peace and harmony
that we feel within ourselves when we are in sexual union
with another affects the peace and harmony in our homes,
in our work and in the world around us. The kabbalists
even say that the ecstasy one feels when God is involved in
human intercourse is but a foretaste of the world to come.

When your encounter is loving, you are the mirror of the King in union with the Shekinah, forming one soul with your partner, God and the universe.[24]

One woman in my group described such an encounter like this: "In the orgasm I could feel this God-energy coming through me. I felt so connected, so open. It was as though someone was speaking to my soul. Everything was beautiful. All things were interconnected, complete and endless, including myself. For a moment in time I felt like I had journeyed beyond the physical world and tapped into the energy of the universe." Another woman, who, unfortunately, could not make this spiritual connection with her husband, said this: "There is an orgasm which is mechanical and an orgasm which is spiritual. It is the difference between feeling filled as opposed to just a release. It's the same difference between people who have sex just to have sex, and people who have sex to go to another level of consciousness." Ultimately, going to that level is a gift to God. I think we should take a hint from a very religious woman who once stopped me as I was concluding a workshop. She wanted to thank me for the work I was doing, so she took me aside and gently whispered into my ear, "The moment before orgasm, I stop and say, 'This is for you, God.'"

That kind of ecstasy may seem unusual, perhaps even unattainable, yet Eve's story implores us to explore the places that challenge our inhibitions and imaginations.

EVE

Eve could have remained naïve and childlike and lived in an oblivious utopian state. She chose instead to walk into a new world and teach us how to fully unite with our partners and with life. Eve left Eden with a dream of how life is meant to be: woman and man equal in partnership, equal in pleasure, equal in the sight of God. As she was forewarned, she warns us by saying, "It is not easy. You must be willing to eat the fruit of knowledge and be comfortable in your divinity, even if it means losing your footing on your own familiar ground by changing jobs, locations, relationships or just attitudes. Then you will be able to nurture new shoots in new gardens and create new forms of paradise wherever you go."

Chapter 4

Jochebed

BIRTHING
MOTHERHOOD

*T*he Israelites had been living fruitful lives in Egypt for several generations when a new pharaoh came into power. As they far outnumbered the Egyptians, the new pharaoh feared they would take over the country if they were not contained. So he ghettoized their camps and enslaved them with harsh labor. To control the population of the Israelites, the pharaoh decreed that all newborn girls could live, but the boys were to be smothered and thrown into the Nile. The Israelite midwives, however, disobeyed the pharaoh. They used the excuse that the children were born too quickly to be counted.

During this time, Jochebed gave birth to a son and kept him hidden from the Egyptian guards for three months. When she could conceal the baby no longer, she wove a basket and placed him in it and set it afloat on the Nile. His sister Miriam lingered in the reeds to see what would happen to him. Pharaoh's daughter came to bathe by the river and heard the baby's cries, and when she saw that the baby was Hebrew, she asked for an Israelite nursemaid. Miriam brought her mother to the princess, and Jochebed was hired to nurse the baby. When he was weaned, Jochebed brought her son to Pharaoh's daughter, who then adopted him and called him Moses, which means "to draw out" (Exodus 2:10). Moses led his people from slavery in Egypt through the waters of the Red Sea to the land of freedom.[1]

*Then the king of Egypt spoke to the midwives, Shifrah and
Puah, "When you are attending the Hebrew women in
childbirth," he said, "watch as the child is delivered, if it
is a boy, kill him, and if it is a girl, let her live."*

Exodus 1:15, 16

THIS WAS the day. Jochebed's timing had to be perfect,
but she knew just what to do. She discreetly placed her
baby in the basket and set it adrift, much as Isis placed
her infant son Horus adrift on the waters of the Nile;[2] or as
the Indian goddess Cunti set her hero-child afloat on the
waters of the Ganges.[3] With her hands, the hands that had
separated many an infant from its umbilical cord, Jochebed
gently pushed until she could no longer feel the texture of
papyrus stems against her fingertips. The waterproof cradle rocked its way past the tall reeds to where she knew
Pharaoh's daughter would soon come to bathe. Jochebed
lifted her face, straightened her spine, exhaled fully, set her
sight northward and walked home. Her young daughter
Miriam stayed and hid behind the reeds at the river's edge.

In her darkened slave quarters, Jochebed bowed her
head, folded her aching body and prayed with the same fervor with which she had labored and delivered. She had

midwived many babies and knew the pangs of labor and delivery well. Yet this child was different. He was the third of her womb and born into danger. She had to save him. And she did. From his first breath, she carefully muffled his cries and concealed his tiny body in the folds of her garment, over her breast. Three moons passed, and Jochebed eluded Pharaoh's guards as they feverishly attempted to sniff out her boy's existence. As her voice cried in prayer, she recalled the long hours she sat weaving the cradle with an anxiety that she could still feel throbbing in her heart. One by one, she would weave her prayers into the stems of the Egyptian water plants so they would protect her tiny baby when it would be time for her to let him go. Now all she could do was wait as the cradle rocked its way over the waters of the Nile. She was sure that her baby would be safe. Yet there was still the gnawing pain of separation.

Outside, the sun had changed its course. Inside, moments seemed endless. Jochebed, immersed in prayer and mesmerized by recent memories, never heard the creak of the door as it opened to the light. It was Miriam. "Mama! Mama! Pharaoh's daughter wants to see you!" Pantomiming with her young girl's exuberance, Miriam reenacted the princess's discovery of the baby, and how she—Miriam—sauntered over to the place where the princess was with her entourage and saw the guarded curiosity and the tenderness with which the princess lifted the child from the cradle. When Miriam saw that the princess was taken with the child and heard her wonder aloud who would nurse him, she innocently asked, "Shall I go and find you a nurse-maid among the Hebrew women?" Miriam then showed Jochebed how she nervously held her breath until the moment the princess said, "Go and find a woman to nurse this child." And Miriam, trying to keep calm, walked until she was out of sight of the entourage. Then she sprinted through the bushes, on the dusty desert roads, until she arrived home to rejoice with her mother. "The baby is safe! The baby is safe! God is with us!"

It was not always this dangerous in Egypt, nor were the Israelites always slaves.

And Pharaoh spoke to Joseph saying: Your father and brothers have come to you in Egypt, take the best of the land and let your father and brothers live there, and those who are strong, appoint them rulers over my cattle.

Genesis 47:5, 6

When Joseph, the favored son of Rachel and Jacob, was in the pharaoh's court, the Israelites were treated as royalty.

JOCHEBED

As the story is told, Joseph was sold into slavery by his jealous older brothers.[4] After unfortunate episodes as a slave and a prisoner in Egypt, Joseph gained a reputation as an excellent interpreter of dreams, which brought him to the attention of the ruling pharaoh. Interpreting one of Pharaoh's dreams, Joseph predicted there would be seven years of plenty and then seven years of famine in Egypt. Pharaoh was so impressed with Joseph's honesty and wisdom, he appointed him head viceroy and gave him dominion over all the royal lands and finances.[5]

However, when Joseph died and a new pharaoh came to power, the successor became paranoid about the growing numbers of Israelite citizens. He complained that they multiplied too quickly and feared they could possibly take over Egypt by their numbers alone. Instead of befriending the Israelites and keeping them on his side, this new pharaoh enslaved them and condemned them to hard labor, to brick making with inadequate resources. When this plan for population control failed, he decreed that all newborn males be smothered at birth and thrown into the Nile.

At first, havoc reigned in the Israelite camps. Jochebed's husband, Amram, was a respected leader amongst the men, and all eyes were on him for direction in this crisis. He was so overwrought about Pharaoh's threat that he decided all the Israelite men should divorce their wives in order to prevent childbirths that would result in death. The men left their homes and lived separately from the women. With each day, their morale lessened, until one evening, as the men were drifting aimlessly in the marketplace, exhausted from building and making and hauling the huge bricks, grieving over their divorces, a voice rose amidst the dispirited crowd—the voice of Miriam. According to the Talmud, Miriam said to Amram: "Father, your decree is worse than Pharaoh's. Pharaoh's decree to kill the Israelite newborns is only directed against the males. But yours is directed against everyone—both males and females!" Miriam showed Amram that he was acting like a coward in the eyes of God by whimpering at the feet of Pharaoh. The women heard about Miriam's remark and rejoiced amongst themselves over her forthrightness and bravery. Amram reconsidered, returned to Jochebed with the passion of a new groom, and they re-wed.[6] Following Amram's lead, the men re-wed their wives, inspired to be courageous rather than intimidated.[7] And according to the Zohar, in Miriam's honor, that day is continuously commemorated in the heavens by those who were part of the generation who wandered in the wilderness with Moses and is called "the day of the marriage celebration." (Zohar 3:163a)

Jochebed had a special perseverance that, no matter how awkward or perilous things may have been, enabled her to not only endure but improve the situation. Jochebed herself was a child born in transition, conceived when her parents were trekking the arduous road from Canaan to Egypt not so many years before. As their caravan approached the walls of the city, her mother's water broke and Jochebed was born at the gates of Egypt.[8] A new child in a new land, born with a destiny to fulfill. Kabbalah teaches that each child is born with a unique mission and a distinctive gift with which to enhance the world. The fact that Jochebed was born at the gateway between Canaan and Egypt was symbolic of her own life's mission, which was to become a midwife to a generation born into the slave pits of one country and rebirthed with freedom into another. In the Bible, we read that the midwives to whom Pharaoh made his proclamation were called Shifrah and Puah.[9] The Midrash Rabbah explains that they were in actuality Jochebed and her daughter, Miriam. When Jochebed was on duty as a midwife, the people called her by the name Shifrah, which means "one who is pleasant or beautiful," because regardless of the danger outside, she helped the mother breathe calmly and created serenity for the ritual of birth. They called Miriam, Puah, which means "to bring one to life by breathing," because she was responsible for ensuring the first breath of the infant, the breath that gives the child life.[10] Jochebed's children, Miriam, Aaron and Moses, were her gift to the world.[11] The Zohar says that God endowed each of Jochebed's children with a gift to the Israelites: with Miriam came a bottomless well, with Aaron came the clouds of glory and with Moses came the manna, or bread from heaven. These mainstays of water, shade and food sustained the Israelites during their trek through the desert.[12] The Israelite women knew they were in God's hands when this mother-daughter team arrived to bring light into their dim slave houses.

With Miriam assisting, Jochebed gave birth to Moses. To Jochebed, the womb was a part of her body that was filled with spirit; she could feel God's presence there, ordaining the blood that flowed through her veins. She was already three months pregnant when Pharaoh made his decision, and inside her an embryo was preparing to grow into a leader of Israel. Kabbalah teaches that each child is a spark of God that brings new light to the world, and the Zohar says that the world came to be when the heavenly forces brought forth two children—heaven and earth.[13] Jochebed must have felt that the birth of Moses was another cosmic event. The rabbis say that when Moses was born, the house was flooded with light,[14] light radiating from both Moses and Jochebed, whose name means "glory of God." Jochebed drew Moses out of her womb as Pharaoh's daughter would later draw him out of the water, and he would eventually, with Miriam and Aaron, lead the Israelites through the Red Sea and into the promised land.

In Jochebed's life we see a woman whose ardent faith in

her God, a force that no one could enslave, helped her maintain control over her own body and life, as well as those of the other women in the slave pits who experienced her caring midwifery. She shows us that you can turn chaos into a sanctuary, and a time of labor into moments of nurturing.

Every mother would like to think her child is a messiah of sorts, someone who will bring healing and peace to the world. Yet what I found in speaking with many women over the years was that women thought of childbirthing mainly as a bodily function, an event that has little to do with beauty, ritual or awareness that with each child we are birthing a new light of God, just as Jochebed did when she birthed Moses. For some women, delivery was peaceful and joyous, but for others it was fraught with fear and pain. As one woman said, "Suddenly I didn't have anything to do with my body. I had given birth to a child, and the doctor had taken charge of my body, my sex life and even my decisions about mothering. Now, twenty years later, I'm learning to reclaim my body. How I wish I could birth all over again, consciously." A younger woman who had a cesarian explained, "With the first child I was going to do it naturally. But when they said it was going to be surgery, I was completely thrown off guard and lost control. I just never counted on the possibility. I lost control. But up until then it was perfect. I was planning my childbirth. I was having the people I wanted in the room with me, the right music, prayers, fragrance and colors. I was going to have the baby stay with me, breast-feed and the whole nine yards. It all happened exactly that way—the next time."

How can we make birthing a spiritual experience? Every woman knows it is a miracle, but in the urgency of the moment too few are alert to the power and holiness of the process. Most parents have enough to do just counting to make sure they see all ten fingers and toes, let alone pausing to say a prayer of thanks. Many husbands are counting deep and short breaths with their wives on the labor table, not conscious of the angels that are flying around the room. How many women do you know who think of God or spirits when they have their feet up in stirrups and their vaginas stretched to the limit, up close and in their doctor's face?

Granted, the commotion in modern delivery rooms is not as adverse a condition as those that prevailed in the slave pits, though we can learn from Jochebed's approach to childbirth. Since the beginning of time, midwives were referred to as wise women and healers. They had a spiritual bond with the mothers and with the children they carried from the womb into the world. Jochebed and her Israelite sisters in Egypt were part of this breed of women, healers and midwives. As they toiled in the hovels of enslavement, these midwives were probably also savvy to the lurking dangers from the guards. They knew how to conceal pregnant bodies, hide infants from peril and breast-feed on the run. They did not knuckle under to any pharaoh or guard. Their strength and pride came from an abiding faith in a God they could not see yet knew existed within and beyond themselves. They believed their lives had a purpose—to deliver a generation from slavery into freedom.

If I could do it all over again, which I won't, but if I could, I would choreograph my children's births like a colleague of mine did, and attempt to infuse that act with the same awareness of God's presence that the Israelite women had. My colleague gave birth in the privacy of her own bedroom at home. She described it by saying, "While I was pregnant I meditated on the perfect environment for birthing my child into this world. As the elements came to me, I created it. My bedroom became the sanctuary, with my bed symbolic of an the altar. All my loved ones surrounded me with prayers. The music playing alternated between Gregorian chant, instrumental music and prayers that we all chanted together. My brother videotaped and my sister-in-law assisted the midwife. Everyone helped me relax and stay calm, rubbing my feet with aromatic oils and patting my head with cold compresses. My daughter came into this world amidst the glory of Pachelbel's *Kanon in D,* into the loving embraces of all present. It was truly miraculous."

I never forgot that story, and when my own dear friend

went to a birthing clinic at a local hospital, we tried to re-create that spiritual setting for her. She was invited to se-lect three people who could be with her at the birthing. She selected her husband, of course, and her two close friends, a female chiropractor and myself, a rabbi. As she was settling into the birth room, we were excitedly assisting her in get-ting situated in the new environment. The nurse, who seemed spiritually attuned with us, came in and was very helpful, informing everyone as to the procedures. We ad-justed the viewing mirrors, joked and then prayed. The room was abuzz with love and excitement before the doctor came in.

My friend's contractions were arriving closer together in time, and she felt that with one good push, the baby would come out. At which point the nurse yelled abruptly, "Don't push! The doctor isn't here yet. You have to wait for the doctor before you can do anything." The doctor was in the hospital, he just wasn't in the room yet. The nurse didn't mean to jar us; she was only doing her duty. But I am sure Jochebed did not have to wait for a doctor before she could do what came naturally—in fact, the women in the He-brew camps often gave birth before the midwives arrived.[15] But since the nineteenth century, when mainly male doc-tors overtook the midwife trade, it has become a different story.

The joy in the room sobered, my friend's easy contractions became tense and an all-pervading apprehensiveness entered the room. As the baby's head was beginning to make its way out of the vagina, the doctor entered the room. The birth mother introduced each of us as her family. He was clearly uncomfortable and asked the other female friend and me to walk into the hall with him. There he informed us that we had to decide which one of us was to remain in the room, because he did not know that there would be two women in addition to the father. This was not in the plan, he told us, but he would've admitted us both if this was written on his chart. I felt as if I were standing in the court of Solomon being asked which half of the baby I wanted. There was such a familiar ring to this bizarre occurrence, as if we were in some Elizabethan drama with a story line of woman pitted against woman.

We refused to make a choice. Either we both remained in the room, or we both stayed in the hall. At which point the doctor repeated, "You should have told me. If you wanted to make this a spiritual experience, I had to be informed. I had to be in on the planning." At which point we reminded him that there was a baby about to be born and pleaded with him to stop the caviling and just get back inside and help birth the baby. He self-righteously marched into the birth room. Through the door we heard him ask our friend, "You have to decide which woman you want in this room." In her stupor she said, "I want them both." He returned to the hall, and as a policeman would escort a felon, escorted us back into the birth room and instructed us not to say a word. So we went in quietly, remained stone-still and silent, witnessing what we had hoped would be a beautiful experience of welcoming this child into the universe. Instead, we were like two mice hiding in the corner as the big cat dominated the scene. Regardless of this doctor's insensitivity, he could not detract from the fact of a new daughter being born into the world. A sister. A mother.

The mother of a friend of mine, a newly sworn-in American, experienced a similar struggle. On the eve of February 12th, 1949, Lincoln's birthday, this woman walked into the kitchen, belly nine months full, and announced to her husband, "This baby is going to be born tonight." Her husband, who barely spoke English, was not ready to argue with her, so he immediately took her to the hospital. There the doctor abruptly dismissed her remark and turned to the husband and said, "No way is she going to give birth tonight. Go home. I'll give her something so she can relax, and you can come back in the morning to pick her up." As the husband was on his way out of the hospital, the woman's water broke and she gave birth right there in the hospital bed.

As I look back on this, I think of how we women have lost control of our own bodies. It seems as if in the delivery

118

room, science often supersedes a history of woman's intuitive approach to this process. In this time of hospitals endeavoring to create more hospitable environments, medical schools need to train doctors to be more sensitive and spiritually oriented. God's energy plays through us, so we need not play at being God. Jochebed did not pretend to play God, rather, her courage came from letting go of her ego, which allowed her to empower the mothers, not overpower them. With the strength of a warrior, Jochebed battled ignorance and vulnerability with faith and tenderness.

Still, there are some doctors who, like the midwives before them, know the heart of a woman. There was a doctor, an older woman—interestingly enough, called Dr. Angel—who brought many children into this world. One of her patients, a woman in my group, relayed this about her: "When this doctor helped me birth my daughter, she cried with us. It was such a beautiful bonding between the doctor, my husband and myself."

Though men may be either present or absent during the birthing process, they need to be available during the child-rearing stages. Jochebed birthed on her own, but she would not parent her children alone. Had Jochebed and Amram's relationship been based only on procreation, Miriam could not have convinced Amram to return to her parents' marriage bed. Jochebed and Amram's destiny was to partner each other,[16] not only in raising children, but in living a fully sexual, fully passionate life. They needed to reunite because they could not afford to lose the passion they shared. So often I counsel couples who have had passionate love affairs before they were married. Then as soon as the kids come, zip. Their passion is dead. They give their lives over to their children, and somewhere along the way they find they have nothing left to give to each other except lonely nights and stale conversations.

Parents at the moment of conception open a channel for something new to take place in this world. The hopes and dreams they plant in the newborn together, they also plant within each other, creating a new level of optimism. If all their energies are focused only on the newborn baby, then they are missing out on the mystery. The Talmud states that there are three in the creation of a child: God, the mother and the father.[17] Let me illustrate the bonding of these three partners with this example. A sage gives you two jewels and shows you the magic light with which you can take the two jewels and turn them into three. Now that you have the three jewels, you'd like to thank the sage for gifting you with the magic light that increased your treasure. So you take very good care of the third jewel but in the process forget the two that helped the third one come into being. The sage is like God, whose magical light is meant to shine on all three jewels, not just one, each jewel attaining its full radiance in the reflection of the others.

When parents concentrate only on fostering a shine in their children, they miss the full radiance that is possible when they include themselves.

With wisdom a house is built.

Proverbs 24:3

There are times, no matter how helpful partners are in caring for each other and their children, when a woman needs some solitude. In Exodus 1:20 we read that "God was good to the midwives and the people increased in number and became very strong." And Exodus 1:21 continues: ". . . because the midwives feared God, [God] made them houses." As we take a closer look at the Hebrew in these verses, we can retranslate the word for midwives, *miyaldot,* to mean "the women who brought children into the world"; the word *yaru,* "they feared," to mean "they would see"; and the word for God, *Elohim,* to mean "the Gods," implying that all the women who brought children into the world could see the many images of God within each one, and these women were gifted with their own houses. To some biblical translators a "house" means a household, a dynasty or a family of one's own. For example, in Jeremiah 21:12 King David's dynasty is referred to as the "house of David." But I think it means an actual dwelling place where a mother could find silence, solitude and comfort, as described in Psalm 68:7: "God creates a house for those in solitude." Every mother yearns for moments of solitude and relief from the daily chores. A working mother in a single-parent household especially needs somewhere to relax undisturbed—a room of her own in which to sit and think clearly, or to do nothing at all without feeling guilty. As a woman in my group remarked, "Every time I leave my kids with a baby-sitter, just so I could go out and have some fun, I feel guilty." Or as another woman in the group, an overachieving attorney, said, "When I stay home I feel guilty I'm not working, and when I'm working I feel guilty I'm not home with the kids." In her book *A Room of One's Own,* the writer Virginia Woolf wrote that in order to create, women need some space and time away from everyday demands. But you don't need to be an artist to acquire a room of your own. Everyone who has the courage to grow must have one. For some women, the bathroom becomes the only place of peace to which they can retreat. So they sit in a warm, soothing bubble bath while their children are being watched by another. For others, a room of their own means getting out of the house into the world and seeing life from an adult perspective.

I think of the painter Georgia O'Keeffe who left her husband, photographer Alfred Stieglitz, and moved from the crowded city of New York to the isolation of Abiquiu in New Mexico. This was a bold act for a woman, especially in the early part of this century. Her marriage stayed intact, while her spirit and her talent grew in the open spaces of the desert wilderness. Every day she would shlep huge canvases and heavy supplies into the wilds and capture the erotic topography of the land. And there are women artists I know today who have rented space outside of their homes in order to be in an environment free from distraction so that they can create. In my own life, I too have found that in order to write books I have had to leave home and be in solitude. During the heaviest writing periods, I work away from home during the week and return only on the weekends. I am sure this is a lifestyle that my mother would have found luxurious.

Now that my children are grown, I often think of the times I needed a room of my own. In hindsight, I would like to say to mothers that money spent on child care is as good an investment as money in the bank. The return earned from child care is invaluable immediately, whereas the interest you accumulate in the bank isn't going to be worth much in years ahead if your child only sees you overanxious, overwrought and overtired. Spend the money and sit in the tub, go to the movies or take a walk by the ocean. Sometimes you can't afford *not* to have a baby-sitter. Do it, even for one hour a day. And if you feel guilty, think of the good guilt mentioned in chapter 3. Remember, if your luster goes dim, no one else is going to come by and polish it for you. God is waiting to play with you in your own treasure-house—a space where you fantasize and dream, where you are most inventive, playful and free. Some younger mothers still smirk or giggle when I mention treasure-house, fantasize, play and God in the same sentence. That is because once they have their own children, they are bogged down with responsibilities at home and at work, and they don't believe they can access the child within themselves and they consider such an idea a waste of time. If we do not give ourselves permission to seek God out at all, let alone imaginatively, our children are left bereft of the joys that present themselves when we do—and who else will show them how to give themselves permission if we don't?

Acknowledging the child within as a spirited expression of the Divine can do more than help women to be better mothers—it may help us to honor the adult who gives life. When a child is born there is much ado about the baby and little, if anything, celebrated about the mother's nine months of pregnancy, labor and delivery. We need to continue to create celebrations to honor the fact that a woman's body, mind and spirit are transformed and sometimes shocked by conception and birth. To celebrate motherhood in my group, I spent one evening leading a visualization where each woman imagined she was giving birth to the child within herself. She saw herself coming into this world as a newborn, welcomed with pomp and celebration and accompanied by the angels and embraced in the arms of loved ones. She heard the chanting of Psalm 2:7: "Today you are born anew in God," and saw herself as a freshly created image of God, brought to the earth with unique gifts to give. Then each woman visualized herself growing through the years, taking pride in herself both as a mother and as a child. This was a liberating experience for the women, and many of them remarked how calm—yet energized—they felt, being able to celebrate the pure, carefree girl within them along with the responsible parent.

This visualization was conceived to help these women realize the possibilities and joy in motherhood, and to put its normally one-dimensional depiction behind them. For in the process of our own birth-giving events, we develop a part within ourselves that knows when to contract and when to expand, when to hold back and when to give forth, when to play and when to parent; when to be available and when to retreat in solitude. As we seek to find these balances, we can look to Jochebed's story for guidance. With strength and focus, despite the dangerous climate, she delivered her own children and kept them safe, for she knew that they would deliver the next generation out of the narrows of slavery into freedom. We too can gain a new perspective of what it means to keep our faith while gaining control over our own bodies, maintaining passion with our partners and living with purpose and meaning. Perhaps, most importantly, we can understand that just as the child is a miracle of life, so too is the birth-giver.

Chapter 5

Deborah

BIRTHING
A WOMAN'S LIFE

*D*eborah, the Israelite judge, lived during the period when her people were cruelly oppressed by the reign of Jabin, king of Canaan, and his brutal military captain, Sisera. Since no one else was acting on Israel's behalf, Deborah sent for the military commander, Barak, to help her wage war against Israel's oppressors. Barak insisted she join him in battle, or he would not go. So Deborah accompanied him and they led ten thousand volunteers to join in the war against Sisera's mighty army of nine hundred chariots and the multitudes who accompanied them. Although the Israelites were outnumbered, Deborah prophesied that not only would they win, but Sisera would be delivered to Israel by the hand of a woman. During the later stages of the battle, as the Israelites were defeating the Canaanites, Sisera escaped to the tent of Jael, the wife of a metalworker. Jael drugged him, then hammered a peg through his head. Jael delivered Sisera's dead body to Barak, and the Israelites' triumph brought about the decline of the Canaanite kingdom.[1]

And she sat under the palm tree of Deborah, between Ramah and Beth-El in the hill country of Ephraim; and the children of Israel came up for her advice.

Judges 4:5

THE MAIN roads were no longer accessible.[2] They were blocked by the iron chariots of the cruel and oppressive Sisera. If you wanted to seek Deborah's counsel, you had to journey the alternate routes when going into the hills of Ephraim in the southernmost part of the Canaanite kingdom. There, on the road between Ramah and Beth-El, you would have turned onto the small footpath and walked through the olive orchards and palm trees. You would have seen a stately woman, seated beneath the firm, long fronds and clustered fruit of a date palm. You wouldn't have been surprised to wait in the long line, for many traveled the dangerous terrain for a word of wisdom, a look of compassion or an exhortation to courage from the wise Deborah. No one hurried. Some brought picnic lunches and sat in the shade of the orchards until she was ready to receive them. But all walked away invigorated with renewed faith and resolutions to their dilemmas.

Today Deborah's mind was troubled by the horrendous tales of cruelty she was hearing. One by one, the people described hardships suffered at the hands of the Canaanite king, Jabin. His men were destroying the farmers' fields, raping and abducting the women and killing the children. The people felt helpless, paralyzed by their own fear because they were outnumbered and outmuscled and outweighed by Canaan's politicians, soldiers, chariots and weaponry.

What could Deborah, judge and prophetess, do to alleviate the oppression of her people? How could she break through the dread and debilitation of generations of oppression? As you drew closer and listened to the impassioned counsel of the stately woman sitting under the palm tree, you couldn't have helped but notice that the gestures and the words you heard were coming from a source beyond herself. It was Deborah's deep faith in the spirit of God that was within her that gave her the wisdom and courage to rescue her people.

These problems provoked Deborah, who smelled war. She began to fight back by calling on Barak, her trusted commander. Some medieval commentators associate Barak with Deborah's husband, Lappidoth, because the two names are so similar in meaning. The word *barak* means "lightning" and Lappidoth comes from the root word *lappid,* meaning "flame."[3] The Talmud teaches that in order to avert doom, change one's destiny or acknowledge a spiritual awakening, one adds on a new name.[4] When Deborah called her husband Barak instead of Lappidoth, she was awakening the spirit within him that not only could emit flames of light, but could also direct it like a thunderbolt in the midst of battle in order to ensure a victory. Deborah encouraged Barak to wage war not for his honor, but for God's, saying: "Didn't God, the God of Israel command you, saying, 'Go and seize Mount Tabor and take ten thousand men . . . and I will take possession of the Kishon river . . . and bring Sisera, his chariots and multitudes to you, and I will deliver him into your hand'?" (Judges 4:6, 7) Because Barak had less confidence in his skills and more confidence in Deborah's abiding faith in God, he responded, "If you will go with me, I will go; but if you will not go with me, I will not go." (Judges 4:8) Now listen to how Deborah answered Barak. She said, "I will surely go with you. However, the journey you are about to take will not be for your honor; for God will give Sisera over into the hand of a woman." Now let me tell you, Sisera, whose name in Hebrew means "battle gear," was no wimp.[5] He was known to be the mightiest man in the world at that time. One medieval commentary, the Midrash Abba Guryon, says that at the sound of Sisera's voice, cities fell and beasts froze in their tracks.[6] Yet it happened exactly as Deborah foretold.

With her confidence in herself and in God, it was no surprise that the people accepted Deborah as the first woman judge in Israel. Judges were not elected by the people but were considered to be sent by God at crucial periods when Israel needed a rescuer to lead the people out of oppression. Ehud rescued the people from the Moabites; Shamgar rescued them from the Philistines; and Deborah led the military coup against the Canaanites. Deborah, like the judges before her, heard the call from God and then revealed God's plan for victory to a nation.

DEBORAH

Deborah and Barak went northward together to collect a volunteer army, and she proved to the people that they could overcome the odds. Not everyone was eager to join them. Some of the tribesmen talked and speculated about the outcome but didn't "walk their talk." Others made as though they were going to join, but stayed behind. Some hid in the waters by their ships, and others on ships that remained at anchor out in the bay. But these doubts and fears did not dampen Deborah's enthusiasm. She moved on with Barak and eventually accumulated an army of ten thousand. Together they journeyed into the hills around Mount Tabor, without chariots and skilled fighters, and with hardly any weapons. This ad hoc army gasped as they watched the heavily armed forces of Sisera moving through the valley and awaited Deborah's next move anxiously, even though they were sure her directions were in tune with God's will.

Faith outwitted muscle and skill in this war. God rained a ghastly storm on Sisera's army, and his nine hundred chariots were bogged down in the mire of the muddy roads. Troops, chariots, horses and soldiers were all sliding and scrambling over each other. As the waters of the Kishon river flooded, they swept the infantry off their feet and obstructed their vision. Swords were flying every which way, and before Sisera's men knew it, they were scalded by their own weapons and dropping like flies.[7] The Zohar states that Deborah knew she could connect directly to God in order to bring down the heavenly waters of renewal.[8] Kabbalah teaches that when people like Deborah open themselves up to being a channel for God, their pure intentions can cause these heavenly waters to descend, intermingling with the earthly waters, like rain on fertile land. Consequently, in the Jewish tradition, rain is considered a sign of good fortune, and the Zohar refers to Deborah as the "Mother of Israel"—not because she gave birth to children, but because she brought Israel from destruction to life.[9]

As the Israelites were claiming their victory, Sisera fled to the tent of Jael. Jael and her husband were artisans, independent spirits, keeping to themselves, living on the outskirts of Kedesh. Well aware of the struggle of the Israelites, she kept a guarded watch on the attack as she helped her husband file the metal for the tent pegs, hammers, spears and knives they sold in the city. When Sisera appeared at her tent door, panting for help, she agreed to assist him. She fed him milk. And when he settled into a sound sleep, Jael gingerly lifted one of the sharpened pegs and, with a swift movement, hammered it through Sisera's head. By the time Barak reached her tent in search of his enemy, Sisera was already dead, delivered, as Deborah had said, into the hand of a woman.

They may never have met, but Deborah and this courageous woman were kindered spirits. And in fact, in the

Midrash, Rabbi Huna refers to Jael as a judge.[10] Deborah was a creative spirit, and she probably enjoyed the company of writers, musicians and artisans like Jael and her husband. Jael, like Deborah, didn't need to live in the hubbub at the center of town. She was satisfied on her own quiet property, where she was free to live and create as she wanted. Though the Hebrew word *jael* means "mountain goat," the root letters *ayin, lamed, hey* in different formations could also mean "to go up" or "to accomplish."[11] Untamed, quick, and not afraid of slippery slopes or soaring heights, Jael focused on her goal and surmounted whatever obstacles were placed in her path.

Nowhere do we hear Deborah speak about a wealthy father, brother or husband. Whatever Deborah had, she created through her deep faith and trust in God and in herself. She embodied the nurturing of a many-breasted goddess, like Artemis at Ephesus, who feeds the world. She was a homemaker, a farmer and a candlestick maker, as well as a prophetess, judge and sacred warrior. She amassed fertile land holdings and financial fortune.[12] By the time she became a judge in Israel she was financially set for life. She didn't have to work. She didn't have to do anything. She could have spent her days primping, charting her finances and overseeing her orchards. But Deborah thrived on encouraging independence in others.

As we circle her landscape, we can explore the nature of

Deborah's creativity and success, and find the secrets to fostering independence in our own lives. Everyone has a talent and the need to know how to use it. Some women I know sit at home, or in a windowless office cubicle, praying each day that someone will come along and help them find that talent. They look at the men who pass by and wonder, is this going to be my knight in shining armor? Is this the man who is going to rescue me from labor and toil and make me a princess? Make me whole? And in the meantime, their lives become a bore. They might as well be sitting at a table in a soda shop, waiting with a malted and two straws for Mr. Right to come along. Sitting and waiting is not going to change your life. Pay close attention to your inner voice, regardless of outside influences or doubts, and then, when you are no longer searching for it, you will hear a validation.

In Deborah's name we can unlock more secrets to finding our own purpose. The root letters of the name Deborah, *daled, beit* and *resh,* in different formation can mean "to arrange, speak, motivate and litigate." The word *deborah* in Hebrew means "bee," which may not be a coincidence, because Deborah, in a way, was her own queen bee. It is possible too that Deborah's name was an homage to the Mycenaean and Anatolian winged goddesses of the Hittite Empire, which were actually bees known by various names. Bees have a rich history of symbolizing female power. They were the goddesses of the Amazon warrior-priestesses who defended their homeland against foreign invaders.[13] In Greek mythology, Melissa, the priestess to Aphrodite, was the prized "Queen Bee"[14] who procured honey to sweeten the taste and preserve the body. In the ancient matriarchal culture, the feminine secretions blood and honey were considered the elixir of life, made by Aphrodite and her bees to keep the gods alive.[15]

Bees also had another close connection to feminine power and to a female milestone. In Greek they were called *hymenoptera* because they have veiled wings; that word is the ancient source for the word "hymen," which originally meant the veil that covered the inner shrine of Aphrodite's temple. When a man or woman entered that sanctuary of love, he or she lifted and passed beyond a veil that represented the thin membrane that guarded the access to the birthing center of a woman's body and symbolized the power center of a woman's life.[16]

Today, breaking through the hymen is symbolized at a wedding ceremony when the groom lifts the veil of the bride to kiss her. At a Jewish wedding, breaking through the hymen is symbolized by the breaking of the glass, and at a Sephardic wedding by the smashing of a plate. (This act is also a breaking of the figurative umbilical cord that tied the couple to their parents' homes.) In Esther Broner's novel *A Weave of Women,* there is a stirring scene when a mother invents a hymenotomy ritual for her eight-day-old daughter. The purpose of this "piercing the hymen" ritual is to free the daughter from future societal pressures, so that she will not be judged by whether or not her hymen is intact, but by the energy she brings to her life. One of the mother's friends who was attending the ritual, and whose own experience of losing her virginity lacked a sense of sanctity, blessed the baby by saying, "Let your piercing be among friends. Let it be ceremonious and correct. Let it be supervised. Let it be done openly, not in anger, not in cars. . . . how I envy you."

Though we may have already broken through our actual hymens, we still have the opportunity to renew a sense of possibility in our lives. We can consciously lift the veil that prevents us from experiencing and cultivating new pleasures. And this is the scary part for some women, and the exciting moment for others. Once your strings to the past are broken, there is no one or nothing to hold onto. Here is a chance to take all your skills and mother a belief in a source deep within and beyond yourself. Women like Deborah seize the opportunity to be independent, and enthusiastically break their own hymens and lift their wings in order to propel their spirits to greater heights, even if everyone around them is still earthbound.

But for some women, birthing their own life seems like an insurmountable task. Some women stay dependent on

138

men; other women are addicted to outside approval. Many of the women I know eat in order to cope; their bodies blow up like a balloon in frustration and fear. They eat everything. They eat at themselves, they eat the refrigerator, they eat the cupboards. They eat until there's no more room, and then they explode. And what do they have? They have more frustration! Then they use every excuse in the book why they cannot change the pattern. No money; no contacts; no male provider; no health; no time; no energy. No wonder. There are other women, however, who act like marionettes and abandon their power rather than break their strings. Whether homemakers or professional businesswomen, these women abandon their goals when a man or significant other walks into their lives. I know a woman who is powerful and full of spirit. Each time this woman begins a spiritual journey her whole demeanor lifts. She comes alive. But when she shares her growth with her husband, he belittles, criticizes and tries to frustrate her efforts. As a result, she loses her power and stifles her spirit.

For some women, taking a vacation or a spiritual journey, or even a weekend workshop away from their family helps them in breaking their own strings. So often, the women who come to our spiritual spa, LivingWaters, are taking their first step in being independent. They feel free for the first time in many years, probably since their marriages, and they are like birds let out of a cage. If you want to have fun, spend time with a woman who is on her first trip alone. She is effervescent, a little girl in a candy shop to whom everything looks and tastes so good. I remember sitting with a group of women from Alabama, real Southern belles,who came to the spa. On the first day, they were very prim and quite formal. By the second day, they were giggling behind cupped hands, like pots coming to boil but careful not to overflow. Then the third day came, and they were uproariously funny and gregarious. They had the whole dining room in stitches! They had so much fun being themselves without having to worry about their husbands, whom they described as "spiritually frigid." By the fourth day they were already planning their next "all-women's trip."

Who are the happiest and most fulfilled women you know? Probably those who listen to their spirits and turn their dreams into realities. Kabbalah teaches us a way to break through our self-imposed barriers in order to hear our inner voice—the voice of God within us. In the first chapter of Ezekiel, according to kabbalistic interpretation, the prophet illustrates a pattern that can lead one to a direct communication with the spirit of God by describing four metaphoric filters we need to dismantle: a stormy wind, a thunderous cloud, a self-consuming fire and an illusional light. The first filter, the stormy wind that knocks us off our course, may be the conflicting thoughts or relationships that keep us from attaining our goals or even thinking straight. The second filter, the thunderous cloud, is clouded thinking. The way to move through a stormy wind or foggy notions is by becoming relaxed and quiet. The third filter is the fire that rages in misplaced passion. There's a fine line between remaining focused and becoming obsessive. You may, for example, think of nothing but a coveted promotion—only to be devastated when you don't get it. You can stay focused on your goal, however, without being attached to the outcome. The fourth and final filter is the light that calls to us in our weakest moments, when we are most skeptical, and in our brightest moments, when we are most confident. The light will lead you according to your intent. If your intention is darkened by doubt, your path will be dimmed. And if your intention is positive and clear, your path will show you to the light of God.[17] Deborah understood that to hear God's voice she had to step out of her own way and dismantle the inner storms, clouds and fires. When the Israelites cowered at the thought of waging war, she didn't obsess about their fear or let it obstruct her path.

Women are now trying to balance time alone with the time demanded by others. We are trying to work in rhythm with our own inner truths, being available to our families while being available to ourselves as well. This is not always easy, especially for young mothers. Often mothers put aside their own needs until their children are fully grown, or they get a lot of help in order to have a career. One of my friends, an accomplished musician, has a housekeeper to care for her three children. She goes to her studio to compose and record, where she can still her own stormy winds and connect with God in her music. But when she comes home she gets stuck in the doubts and fears of being a "good enough" mother. She is under the illusion that taking over the live-in housekeeper's chores is going to make her a better mommy. So the moment my friend arrives, the housekeeper disappears, and my friend, in a frenzy, cooks up a dinner and hustles her kids around the table. I don't think Deborah would have reacted this way. Deborah would have recognized the attractive auras that surround the images we are told to yearn for, auras that distort priorities and blind us to our own true desires. Instead of relegating herself to the kitchen, she would have sat on the floor and spent the precious time playing with the children.

Too often, we can only see the well-trodden path when we set out to build our lives or to find a life's work. I know a number of women who would love to be their own bosses and financially independent in a job or career that would touch their spirits. When I speak to women who are fulfilled in their careers, I find they often feel that their success is due to the fact that their hearts are involved in their work, and their sense of purpose comes from more than just making money. In fact I know several women who have opted to take jobs where they could express their spirits and satisfy their souls, even though it meant lower pay. In Leviticus 26, God warned the Israelites that when they lost their joy in serving God, their lives would be taken over by estranged authorities that would enslave them.[18] I think that is what has happened to many people. They have lost a sense of purpose, let alone joy, and have given their energies over to people or things that stifle their spirits.

We can begin to understand Deborah's integration of her spirit with her work from a phrase in Judges 4:4, which is usually translated as: "Deborah, the wife [*eshah*] of Lappidoth," but which the Talmud translates to mean "Deborah, a woman of flames," because the Hebrew word *eshah* can mean either "wife" or "woman," and *lappidoth* means "flames." The Talmud continues to explain that "a woman of flames" means that Deborah literally took the fibers of thread and twisted them to create the oil lamps for the Temple sanctuary[19] and turned this product into a lucrative industry. From the profits from these lamps, the Targum Shoftim, a commentary on the Book of Judges, said she amassed a financial fortune, and that is why she did not charge fees for her counseling services.[20] When a woman is fulfilled, she shares it with those around her. This is the way of Deborah. First, there is focus on an intention. Ask yourself, "What do I want?" Not what someone else wants

143

for you. Once you have discerned what you want and it feels right in your soul, then ask: "What do I need to do to get what I want?" Then go for it! Passion moves a woman like nothing else can. Her love for her husband Lappidoth, who was fumbling for a satisfying career, moved Deborah to teach him the skill that generated her fortune, making wicks for the lamps. Lappidoth learned how to twist the wicks for the lamps and built a brisk business on his own.[21] Deborah's love and compassion for others may have moved her to teach the villagers how to twist the wicks also, and with these skills they began their own cottage industry.

There is a woman in my group who loved to give advice, so she turned her peer counseling into a profession and found work coaching corporate executives. Once she felt confident and secure in her career, she began a program to teach others how to do the same. Now several women in the group are professional consultants to corporate clients. One woman entrepreneur in my community saw the need for more public transportation for children, the impaired and the elderly. So she began her own transportation company, but this isn't an ordinary company. Her offices are a sanctuary for people from all walks of life. They have found not only jobs but meaning in caring for the safety of others. When she purchased a new fleet of buses, her office employees, the drivers and her rabbis walked the length of the parking lot, praying for those who would enter the buses.

We prayed for the awareness of the drivers so that they would be conscious that in transporting their passengers they were doing more than driving them to their destinations. They were imparting love. Finally, what we learn from Deborah's victory is best put into excerpts from the Song of Deborah.

When the people let down their hair in Israel,
When they offer themselves willingly,
They bless YHVH.
Listen kings; give ear, princes,
I am to YHVH,
I sing to God.
I will sing praise to YHVH, the God of Israel. . . .
In the days of Jael, the highways ceased,
and the travelers walked through the byways.
The rulers ceased in Israel, they ceased to be.
Until I arose, Deborah.
I arose, a mother in Israel. . . .
And then the land was at peace for forty years.

Judges 5:1–3, 6–7, 31

Deborah and Barak sang this song as they returned from the victory of Israel over Sisera. Some rabbis say that Deborah was arrogant for including herself in the hymn of Deborah. They ask suspiciously, "What did she mean by 'I arose'?" And they answer that it wasn't she but God who arose. Then they mention how dangerous it is to become egocentric and prideful. Some rabbis even say that at the instant she said "I arose," she lost her prophetic abilities.[22] Granted, we do need to be careful not to let our successes or talents go to our heads, for there is always someone waiting around the corner to knock us down a peg or two. Yet Kabbalah teaches that the heavens can only answer you when you call. If there is no call from below, there can be no answer from above.[23] Consider this: The Hebrew word meaning "to arise," *kum,* also means "to awaken." It is a charge from God. In Proverbs 6:9 we are asked: "When will you arise from your sleep?" So we need to accept our victories and be able to share them with others in a way that teaches other women that they too can rise to the occasion when they feel called by God.

Deborah shouldn't be accused of arrogance when many male leaders did what she did. The Bible says that these great men *arose* to do God's bidding, as Joshua did before he went to war,[24] Gideon before he slew the kings of Midian,[25] Saul before he was to be anointed king,[26] David before he slew the Philistines.[27] Think of Moses and Samuel. Moses had a speech impediment—he was tongue-tied—yet the rabbis said that God selected him because he was curious. He didn't take things at face value; he looked beneath, within and around an issue to ascertain its deeper meaning. When Moses saw the miracle of the bush burning without being consumed, he heard the voice of God call out through the fire saying, "Moses, Moses." He responded not from his mind or ego, but from his heart, saying, "Here I am." (Exodus 3:2, 3) When Samuel was still a boy, sound asleep at night in the Temple sanctuary, he heard a voice call out "Samuel, Samuel," and each time he heard the voice he arose and went to the priest Eli, thinking it was Eli who was calling him. The third time Samuel awoke, Eli explained to him that it was God speaking to him, so by the fourth time Samuel heard the call, he was open to responding directly to God and said, "Speak, for I, your servant, am listening." (1 Samuel 3:1–10) Samuel's innocence and openness, like Moses' curiosity, enabled God to speak to him. Moses did not run to put out the fire or call everyone to watch, and Samuel didn't crawl into bed with Eli for fear of evil spirits lurking in the dark. Both rose to the occasion of being summoned by God. Though to most they probably seemed unfit for the job, Moses being tongue-tied and Samuel but a child. And Deborah was a woman in a patriarchal culture. But to hear the voice of God requires only a willingness to step outside of our own limitations and be curious and still enough to see the fire in the bush, or awaken during our sleep. What Deborah was saying was: "There were no rulers willing to take the responsibility. I didn't need to ask permission. I saw a void, and I arose as a mother in Israel." She led her people to an awakening that changed not only herself but the course of history.

What we learn from sitting beneath the sturdy fronds of Deborah's date palm is that whatever we do needs to be an expression of our spirits, and that we must spread our veiled wings before we are bound to a truth that is not ours. But the path you take to find your truth may not be the road that is open. Like those on the path to Deborah's orchard, you may need to travel an alternate route that takes you through hidden valleys and along narrow footpaths. But at the end there will be blessings, as the prophet Isaiah declared: "Arise, shine, for your light has come, and the glory of God is rising like the sun on you." (Isaiah 60:1)

Chapter 6

Miriam

CHANGING
SEASONS

While the Israelites were camped in the wilderness, on their way to the promised land of Canaan, Aaron and Miriam spoke against their younger brother, Moses, about his Cushite wife. They declared that Moses wasn't the only one with whom God spoke, for they too had heard the voice. God was listening to their conversation when, suddenly, all three of them heard God, and they went to the Tent of Meeting, where God called to them. There God explained that some people could hear God through dreams and allegories, but Moses could hear God directly. God was angered and drew near the outside of the tent, and at that moment Miriam's skin turned white with leprosy. Aaron turned around, and, astonished by what had happened to Miriam, apologized to Moses for speaking foolishly and sinfully about him. Aaron pleaded with Moses not to let Miriam die, and Moses cried out to God, "Please heal her." Then God told Moses that Miriam's shame warranted that she be taken out of the camp for seven days, but afterwards she could return to the people. So Miriam was secluded, and the Israelites did not journey forward until Miriam returned to the camp.[1]

And they {Miriam and Aaron} said, "Has God only spoken to Moses? Has God not also spoken with us?" And God heard.

Numbers 12:3

IT ALL started that fateful day when Miriam and Aaron decided to speak with their brother Moses about his marriage. They had noticed that as Moses' influence and charisma increased, the life of his wife Zipporah had begun to darken and dim. Miriam did not want to meddle into Moses' personal affairs, but she knew that she could help his marriage. Miriam knew that Moses' wife, Zipporah, was going through a troubling time, as she herself had and as all women in the changing seasons of their lives do. Zipporah was at that difficult point between youth and age. Miriam understood that, with support, Zipporah's spirit could soar, but without it her spirit might drown. Miriam knew it. Aaron, her older brother, knew it. Moses, their younger brother, needed to learn it. And God was listening.

What was God hearing? A conversation of the heart shared between a sister and two brothers about the charismatic leader's need to give his wife loving attention. Yet they hardly spoke. They didn't have to, for the three of them were joined in a deep meditative state. The presence of God was with them, and they were telepathically connected.[2] Miriam recalled the traditional lighting of the candles when a leader was appointed or promoted to any office, and Zipporah's remark: "Woe to the wives of such leaders for their husbands are no longer available to them." (Yalkut Shimoni, Beha'alotcha 738) The fact that Moses was so attractive physically probably added to Zipporah's frustration. Though the text in Numbers 12:3 reads "Moses was the *humblest* of all men," he was, as the Midrash explains, so ravishingly handsome that everyone loved to gaze at his beauty.[3]

You may say this was an inconvenient time for Moses to be dealing with pampering his wife. After all, he was at the height of his potential as a leader, and everyone revered him as a channeler of God's word. Moses received the word from the Ark of the Covenant in the Tent of Meeting, where a voice would come through the wings of the cherubim that hung facing each other above the ark.[4] The Zohar says that these cherubim, each gazing into the other's face, melted judgment into shades of love and compassion.[5] And just as God dwells in the loving embrace of the cherubim of the ark, so too does God dwell in the embrace of a loving couple. Miriam and Aaron reminded their younger brother of this and of the fact that God did not speak only to him.[6] Moses paused, went silent and listened. Miriam explained to Moses that his wife, Zipporah, as her name indicated, was like a bird—she could be fragile and yet had the potential to soar above and beyond. But her wings had become fettered, and she needed to spread them in order to keep up with the stirrings of change inside her. Miriam knew that Zipporah, like many women today, needed a companion who understood her spirit and could guide her flight. Need they say more?

The Bible says that "God listened" and "spoke suddenly" (Numbers 12:2, 4) to each one individually and summoned them to leave where they were and to go to the Tent of Meeting. Abruptly, and without a word, Miriam, Aaron and Moses arose and walked to where God had summoned them. Then Miriam's epiphany happened.

God came down in the form of a cloud and called Aaron and Miriam to come forward, and God lingered with them. Miriam witnessed the cloud of God[7] drawing nearer and nearer until she was overtaken by the Divine force. Her face turned white, as though she were going to faint. Aaron panicked and thought they had done something wrong. He was afraid Miriam was going to die; her skin looked like that of a stillborn infant. And at that moment something in Miriam did die in the same way that something within Eve died when she ate the fruit of knowledge. And as Eve was reborn, Miriam, in her middle age, was also about to be reborn. She entered into seclusion, retreating to the interior world within herself with God. After a seven-day spiritual communion, Miriam returned renewed. Miriam thanked God and all the celestial beings for gifting her with deeper awareness than she could envision before. In the delicate, warm breeze of the Sabbath dawn, Miriam heard the ancestors and the celestial chorus sing, "Holy, Holy, Holy. You are whole."[8] She returned to her people as a renewed visionary, a healing goddess, a new model of beauty for women in the midst of their lives.

As you've probably noted, this happy ending is nothing like the story told in the beginning of this chapter. The traditional translation of Miriam's story in Numbers 12:1 begins, "And Miriam and Aaron spoke *against* Moses because of the *Cushite* woman he had married; for he had married a *Cushite* woman." The word "against" is derived from the letter *bet,* used as a prefix to Moses' name. The prefix *bet* could also be translated as "with," meaning that Miriam and Aaron weren't challenging their brother, but conversing. This seems more logical since we know from the Talmud that Aaron was peace loving and never spoke against anyone.[9] And the fact that Moses' wife was a Cushite, which in Hebrew also means "dark-skinned," could in this instance be viewed as less of a place of origin and more of a description of color and demeanor. Therefore we could read Numbers 12:1 as, "And Miriam and Aaron spoke with their brother Moses about the circumstances of *his darkened wife,* for the wife he married *had become dark.*"

We are told that God became angry at Miriam for nosing into Moses' private life, struck her with leprosy, changed her and excommunicated her for seven days. As we examine the words in the biblical text, however, we can retranslate them to mean that God heard her inner voice, was proud of her courage and openness and came in to nurture her for the next step in her spiritual journey.

In Numbers 12:9, the traditional version reads, "And God's anger was sparked against *them,* and [God] departed." So right away we see that if God was angry, it was at *them,* meaning it wasn't only at Miriam but at Aaron too. However, the Hebrew word for "anger" and "sparked," *vayechar-aff* could also mean "linger" and "glow." *Aff* is translated as "kindled," "sparked" or "glowed"; the root letters of *vayechar,* which are *yud, chet* and *resh,* also spell out *yachar,* or "to tarry."[10] Perhaps God wasn't angry at all; rather, God's glow lingered as a lover would who had just heard the song of the soul of their beloved. Then in Numbers 12:10, we read, "And when the cloud was *removed* over the tent, behold, Miriam was *leprous,* as white as snow; and Aaron looked at Miriam and she was leprous." Traditionally, the Hebrew word *sar* is translated to mean "remove," but it could also mean "to draw near and around" something. Also, the root letters of the Hebrew word for leprosy, *zadi, resh, ayin,* can also be translated to mean "smitten," as in being overtaken by something.[11] This sentence could read, "And the cloud [of God] *drew near around* the tent, and Miriam was *smitten* and became white as snow; and Aaron turned to Miriam, and behold, she was *smitten.*" Miriam was overtaken in a spiritual epiphany, and her skin became white as snow because she had just seen and touched the likeness of God and felt overwhelmed. When Aaron saw her skin change, he compared it to a stillborn infant's.

But God saved the day. Some say that in Numbers 12:14 God said to Moses, "If her [Miriam's] father were there he would have *certainly spit* in her face, and *she would have hidden* from embarrassment for seven days." Take another look at the Hebrew. The root letters *yud, resh, kuf,* "to spit," could also mean "a green plant" or "bud that flourishes within itself." And the word for "she would have hidden," *tikalaim,* could also be translated from the root letters *kav, lamed, lamed* to mean "she will complete." With this new understanding we can read Numbers 12:14 as "God said to Moses, "*I will bring the bud that flourishes within her to completeness* within seven days; she will retreat outside the camp and then she will rejoin you."

Miriam was God's flower in the desert.[12] She blossomed at a time in her life, at menopause, when people thought it was the beginning of a woman's decline. She was able to tutor Zipporah so that the period in a woman's life we know as menopause became less fearsome. These women inspire us to embrace the changing seasons of our own lives. Through the example of her perseverance, confidence and generosity, Miriam's spirit can shake the dust-covered attitudes that hold us back and can guide us to renewal as God guided her. As we look at her life, we see that Miriam was a model for challenging the status quo and fostering hope.

Aaron loved to make peace between people,[13] and Miriam was never one to hold her tongue. Like Mozart, a child prodigy who played the harpsichord at four, composed music at five and performed in concerts at six, Miriam began voicing her opinions and midwifing as a child of five and prophesied at six.[14] When she was only five, her mother, Jochebed, was called to Pharaoh's court. Miriam accompanied her down an aisle flanked by guards and into the lavish throne room of Pharaoh. He held a decree in his hand and demanded that they obey it, killing at birth all males born to Israelite slaves. Standing before the almighty Pharaoh, Miriam, nose in the air, blurted out that he was evil and murderous. Pharaoh became enraged and would have killed her if Jochebed had not intervened. Miriam's embarrassed and frightened mother appeased and convinced the king to excuse the insolent child because she was too young to understand.[15] Over the years, Miriam's insolence was refined into wisdom and her words were re-

spected. Her father, Amram, who was the leader of the Israelite men, sought his daughter's advice. When she told
him to re-wed her mother and that a redeemer of Israel
would be born to them, instead of rebuking her for her im-
pertinence, he took her before the Sanhedrin, the Israelite
court, where she could speak to all the men and they too
would follow her counsel.[16] Yet, because of her forthrightness, the traditional view makes her out to be a gossiping
shrew, and, traditionally, the biblical texts are translated to
tell the story of an angry God who punishes a woman for
overstepping the boundaries of reserved femininity.

As we look more closely, however, we read in the Bible
that Miriam was welcomed as a prophetess in Israel, and
when she spoke the people knew it was truth. Not only did
the men respect her counsel, but the women also saw her as
their teacher.[17] She helped them to not only hope for but
prepare for a life outside of slavery, and she did this by empowering them to move beyond their fears by not only
confronting change but celebrating it. When Jochebed
placed her baby boy in the Nile, Miriam didn't leave the
site. Instead, she stayed until the Egyptian princess arrived. When she realized that her baby brother was going
to be safe, she came out from behind the tall reeds and
spoke forthrightly to the princess, suggesting a nursemaid
for the baby. Nor did Miriam buckle with fear when the Israelites were escaping from Egypt and reached the edge of

the sea with nowhere to go, pursued by the Egyptian char-
ioteers and their whips. Instead, she took out musical instruments and inspired the women to join her as she
danced her way through the waters as the waves miracu-
lously parted and created a corridor of dry land upon which
they could cross to safety. Miriam understood that passion
and faith can win over fear. And Miriam helped Moses see
that beneath Zipporah's depression there was a wife yearning to renew passionate love between herself and her husband.

What Miriam saw happening in Zipporah, happened in
her, and still happens in menopausal women today. You
wake up in the morning and you feel like an adolescent in
heat. You want passion, and you want to reclaim your life
from missed chances and silences. You feel more awake,
more vibrant and you want more sex.

No, menopausal women are not crazy or loony, or de-
serving of whatever other reductive words people use to describe this complicated state. We are in our prime. But yes,
we can change on a dime. We can cry one minute and laugh
uproariously the next. We can be cold and then hot and
then cold again. Boy, do we get confused and clouded—not
about others, but about ourselves. We look in the mirror
and no matter how many ways we blush our cheeks, color
our lips and arrange our hair, the person in the mirror does
not always look familiar. There are crow's feet, not to men-

tion the sagging breasts, her cheeks are starting to cave in, and her skin—well, what are those spots, anyway?

Our bodies are in flux, our minds are moving rapidly. Many women feel as though they are running out of time and speed up their growth by not waiting for a man or anyone else to give them permission to go ahead and express themselves. For some women the only thing static about their menopausal period may be their family's attitude. Like the woman who told me she entered a new period in her life and started going to night classes in order to learn computers—while her family rebelled because she was no longer sitting at home, cooking their dinners and doing their laundry. Let me tell you some stories of women we probably all know. They climbed to the midpoint of life, then stood ready to fly, but due to their fear of change and lack of support, their feet stayed glued firmly to the ground. Like Zipporah, they faced husbands who were leaders very much in demand in public, yet emotionally unavailable at home. Like Zipporah they had a desire for someone to respond to their life changes, yet lacked support from their own children or parents. Where does all their energy go instead? It bores a deep hole within, crumbles and dies in unfulfilled pleasures, unspoken dreams, unlived lives.

I knew a woman who was practically jumping out of her skin to put a new plan into action. A forty-one-year-old woman who was so full of life. Everyone loved to be with her. She was pretty, smart, talented and successful. For twenty years she played life by her husband's rules. Jane grew the business, chauffered the kids, had dinner ready at six and stayed close to home. She was a perfect business-woman, a perfect mother, a perfect wife. She even sat next to her husband as he held a beer in one hand and the TV remote control in the other. Each night the television dominated the living room—and their lives—from the evening news on, until boredom gave way to sleep.

Then something happened to Jane as it does to many menopausal women. She had a sudden awakening. Her mind, spirit and hormones started coming alive simultaneously, and her family thought she was going bonkers. Her mother told her not to worry, that all women go through this. So she asked her mom, "Well, what did you do when this happened to you?" With hesitation in her voice, her mother admitted that during her menopausal years, she too felt like she was in heat, physically and sexually, and would have loved to have shared it with her husband, but he was emotionally unavailable. "So what did you do about it, Ma?" she asked, and her mother meekly answered, "I became depressed."

That wasn't what Jane wanted to hear. Jane was different. Instead of becoming depressed, Jane took her energy and expressed it. She started reading literature, going to plays and performances, expanding her own mind and exploring her own body. She had so much spiritual energy and romantic fervor, it was hard to come home at night and face the same old thing. She wanted to share this new fervor with her husband. At first Jane fantasized, like numerous women in her situation, about having a love affair with another man. But she opted to have that affair with herself instead by pampering herself with massages, nurturing herself with flowers and gifts and exploring the pleasure centers of her own body.

Another woman who did not have a willing partner with whom she could share her desires took that energy and gave it to a worthy cause. She began to work at an abandoned children's center in her off hours, hugging and rocking babies to sleep. Still another woman I know, also frustrated by the inattentiveness of her husband, rented a hotel room once a month and invited him to visit her there. She would prepare the room with soft lighting, romantic music, fragrant incense and wine in the chalice they had used for their wedding vows many years before. Being in these surroundings, without the kids, the dog and the phone, helped them get reacquainted with each other. At first her husband did it only to placate her, but eventually he too prepared for their evenings at the hotel. He would come with gifts, send notes or flowers or even buy a new robe for the occasion. These rendezvous added the extra excitement they needed to recharge their relationship.

These women discovered what so many of us do—that being hot without a partner who's willing to come trot is like having chicken pox and not being able to scratch. A women is bursting with romance, restlessness and passion. And she is supposed to remain self-contained and demure. Why, when women are in the heat of sexual expectancy, are some husbands so cool? I thought this was a turn-on. Could you please tell the men you know that if they paid more attention to their menopausal partner, all their fantasies could become real? We can be sure that Miriam and Zipporah experienced the sensation of being *in heat*—having the hots *and* the hot flashes; the agony and the ecstasy.

Since a midlife woman has a new sense of bodily rhythm that is no longer associated with monthly menstruation, she can no longer be limited to old patterns of sexuality that were governed by birth giving, contraception or the fact of her motherhood. There is something about not having to worry about being pregnant and all the responsibilities that go along with being a mom that makes a menopausal woman feel sexually liberated. Like Miriam, she now feels free to go where she wants, say what she wants and do what she wants. One woman I know said of this confidence: "I now have a whole new communication with my husband. I tell him just where I want to be touched and what makes me feel good. Now he's more comfortable telling me his needs also. We even started meditating together. When we are spiritually connected, we are so much more sensitive to each other's touch."

So often going through menopause is like a delayed or repeated adolescence. We want to play and have fun, but this time not as naive, dependent children, asking for permission. Women who are going through menopause sometimes change their names, reclaim their maiden name or add on their mother's name. I know several women who had midlife parties and renamed themselves. One woman felt her name was too disempowering and forlorn, and she researched the Native American tradition for a new name. She dropped the name Lorna and took on the name Cheyenne. Another woman in my spirituality group felt her life as Katherine had completed itself, and now she was entering a whole new dimension of living. She took on the name Serenity.

Miriam's names reflected her own ageless enthusiasm. Her most popular name, Miriam, is associated with the ancient goddess Mari, the "Fruitful Mother," who dominated the Holy Land; the Chaldean goddess Marratu; the Persian goddess Mariham and the Christian Mother Mary. *Mir* in Egyptian means "mother love," and the Hebrew word *yam* means "seas"; therefore, we can say that Miriam was the sea mother who lovingly guided the Israelites through the waters, as through a womb, for rebirth.[18] Yet she was also called Naarah, meaning "youthful," because no matter how old she was, she retained the vitality of her youth.[19] She was also called Akharel, meaning "lead dancer"—an acknowledgment of how she danced the Israelites through the Red Sea.[20]

Like Miriam, the women in my group love to dance, and they create every opportunity to let their spirits dance through their feet. When we pray, we dance; when we are at a party, we dance; when we're excited at just being together, we dance. We have the high spirits of girlhood but not the hang-ups about dancing without being asked by a man, or even dancing without any man. Rather than feeling the self-consciousness of our teen years, we are assertive adults. We no longer look at our breasts as appendages we didn't ask for, but as something we carry with honor as we do the lines on our faces. We have the spirit without the awkward discomfort.

I used to think only men talked about sex, but I'm learning that it is a favorite subject with menopausal women. In our girlish boldness, we don't talk only about the physical pleasures of sex, but about how we can care for our partners with our newfound sense of freedom. So often we think our partners have to be just like us, with the same passion, the same desires and the same sense of godliness. But that is not the case. A woman in my group, many years my senior, and who had had several husbands and numerous lovers, once said, "Love them for who they are right now, and then they will be confident to open to new possibilities." I watched this woman with her romances, and she opened up her men as if she were coaxing flowers to bloom. Instead of trying to change my family, I began to do the same. So often we think if we give in to another, we lose. Standing at the midpoint of my life, I've learned, like Miriam, that the more I give from the truth of who I am, not just to be accommodating or out of obligation, the more I receive. And I am never diminished in the process, only elevated.

Just the other day a friend of mine said, "I spent so many years not communicating my needs, that my husband didn't really get to know the true me. Then I went into the 'changes,' and I was so depressed. I walked around feeling torn between thinking I was insanely erotic, or ugly and unlovable. This was because all I wanted was to be touched, but no one did. I cried myself to sleep at night, feeling alone and rejected. What I learned was that although my body was a woman's, inside I was still a little girl. And like a little girl, I was waiting for Daddy to notice me, to hug me, to pick me up. No more, I decided. My husband is now attracted to a woman, not the girl who needs to be taken care of. We are more open, honest, assertive, and more excited to be with each other."

167

Just as we sometimes falsely think that flowers don't grow in the desert, we also think women start disintegrating after fifty. I became fifty last year, and so far, this has been the best year of my life. I can't always explain the ecstasy I feel, I only hear myself repeating to my friends and anyone else interested in hearing, "I'm so glad I'm over fifty!" This feeling of celebration didn't occur overnight. It happened as I settled into menopause, which started in my late thirties. Once I adjusted to hot flashes, decreasing elasticity and increasing sexual desire, I felt freer than ever before.

Each time we enter a new season of life, there is a readjustment period. Seeking spirituality can help us make the transition. The changes that come with menopause can be as profound as Miriam's experience of God, and we may not be able to describe it in a way that others could understand or integrate into their own reality. With this kind of epiphany comes the need for retreat into silence and stillness. Why did Miriam retreat for seven days? What did Miriam do during her seven-day retreat and how did it change her life? Kabbalah teaches that each day of the week embodies a special quality of God. When a person tunes in to these seven qualities of the Divine, he or she becomes more enlightened. You access these qualities through prayer, meditation and infusing them into every thought, word and action. On Sunday, Miriam focused on compassion; on Monday, strength; Tuesday, harmony; Wednesday, success; Thursday, glory; and Friday sexuality.[21] Then on the eve of the seventh day, the Sabbath, she was ready to dip into the well of renewing waters, as pure as a bride renewing her vows with God.

The Talmud likens immersion into the words of Torah to immersion into natural waters, as well as to union with God.[22] The Torah is referred to as "the bride of God," and the eve of Sabbath is when God unites with the bride.

Ablution was common in ancient Egypt, as it was in most ancient religions, from Buddhism and Hinduism to Judaism and Christianity. Complete immersion in a natural body of water was a way of ritually purifying one's intentions. We too can find solace in water—it may not be a lake or the sea, but even taking a leisurely bath is a modern-day equivalent, which allows us to retain the healing power of water in our own daily lives. Today many Jewish people immerse themselves in a natural body of water in a ritual bath, called *mikvah,* which comes from the Hebrew letters *kuf, vav, hey,* and which means "to hope" and "to be confident." Traditionally, this immersion was intended to cleanse a person or object that was deemed to be impure. Kabbalah teaches that each person who lives in the physical world needs to continuously dismantle the filters that mask the light of her or his soul, but that when an object is placed under water, the filters are dismantled.

God assigned Miriam authority over the well of renewing waters—a magical well, first, because it appeared in the desert, the most unlikely place, and second, because it had tremendous healing powers. The water in this well was healing because it sloughed off dead cells and released imprisoned spirits and caged passions. In the Midrash, Rabbi Tanhuma told of a man who was suffering from boils who went to bathe in Tiberias, in a well opposite the middle gate of the ancient synagogue, and was cured. The rabbis said that the well he bathed in was Miriam's Well.[23] Who ever heard of an overflowing cistern in the desert? But wherever the Israelites journeyed in the desert, the magical Well of Miriam emerged from beneath a rock.[24] The Midrash explains that they traveled from one destination to the next, rolling a large cone-shaped rock as part of their caravan of provisions. When they set up camp and erected the Tabernacle, this rock would be placed in the courtyard of the Tent of Meeting.[25] Then the leaders and nobles of the tribes would gather around the stone and sing the song that Miriam wove into the consciousness of the people,[26] the same song she sang by the waters of the Red Sea when God said to Moses in Numbers 21:17, "Assemble the people and I will give them water." Then Israel sang the song:

"Rise up, O well, respond to her. . . ."(Numbers Rabbah 1:4) As the music resonated through the earth, the ground underneath the stone would open and reveal a well of rising water. Miriam's Well is a welcome metaphor for those of us who are traversing our own symbolic deserts—parched with the anxieties that accompany menopause—and yearn to dip into renewing waters that elevate the meaning of this new season in our lives.

Miriam was God's flower that grew out of the desert—a hope for an unexpected flowering and a graceful rising up in our middle years. She was the one who instilled confidence in the Israelite men, who were ready to buckle under Pharaoh's demands. She breathed life into the newborn infants and their mothers. She led the Israelites in dance and music through the Red Sea.[27] They could have looked back and panicked with fear as the chariots of Egypt and the tidal wave followed closely behind them. Yet Miriam directed their gaze forward and handed the women tambourines with which to sing and dance among the thousands who walked to freedom. Through staying conscious of the changes in her own body and spirit, Miriam was able to change the consciousness of her brother, her sister-in-law and an entire nation.

Retranslating Miriam's story elevates her from rebuked gossip to prophetess. In this way Miriam is a model for midlife women. She willingly confronted her changes and celebrated them with passion and dignity. She teaches us to be free even if we have to walk through turbulent waters, for we will reach calmer, healing springs if we let our souls dance to God's timing in our lives.

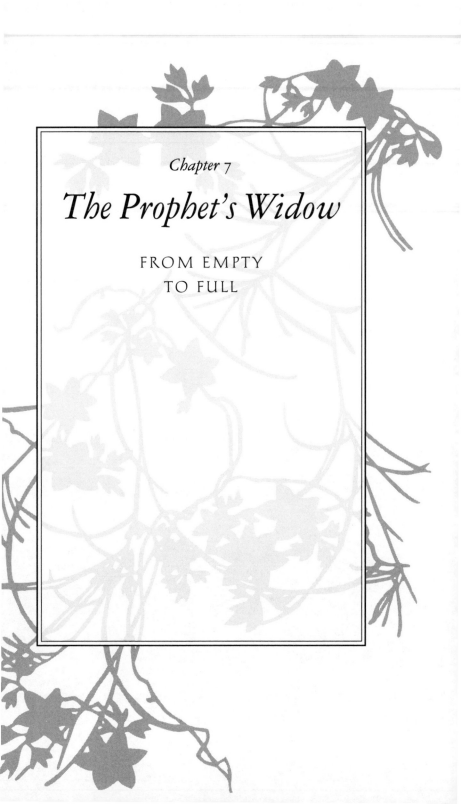

Chapter 7

The Prophet's Widow

FROM EMPTY
TO FULL

*A*fter the war of kings in Moab, when the Israelites returned to Israel, there was a prophet's wife who appealed to the holy prophet Elisha for help. "My husband, your servant, is dead," she told him. "He was a God-fearing man, but now a creditor is coming to take my two children to be his slaves." Elisha responded, "What can I do for you? Tell me what you have in your house." "Nothing," she said, "save a little oil." Elisha told the prophet's widow to go out and collect all the empty vessels she could get from her neighbors, then to bring them into her home and close the door behind herself and her children. When the jugs were safely inside her home, she was to begin filling them with the little oil she had.

The prophet's widow did as Elisha had instructed. As each vessel was filled, she asked her children to bring her yet another. It was miraculous. As long as she had vessels, the oil kept flowing. The moment she filled the last vessel, the oil supply ceased. Then the widow returned to Elisha and reported the miracle of the oil. He told her to pay off the creditor by selling the oil in the vessels, and to live off the profits.[1]

*And a woman, one of the wives of the sons of the prophets,
cried out to Elisha, saying: "Your servant, my husband, is
dead . . ."*

2 Kings 4:1

IT WAS sudden. She had hit rock bottom. No husband, no
money, and, the rumors had it, she would soon be without
home and children, who would be taken into bondage by
the creditors. But she was determined to make it back up.
And she would.

She sat by the last embers of the hearth of a home once
blessed with joy and celebration, stunned by the quickness
of the tragedy. One night she was sleeping tucked beneath
the feather quilt, curled in her husband's embrace. And the
next, she was alone, in despair over her husband's death,
disconnected from her community, a grieving widow one
step away from living in the streets.

She is called "the prophet's widow." We don't know her
real name. But we can intimate something about her experiences. There were groups of prophets and their families
who lived and traveled together. Called "sons of the prophets," they were disciples who congregated around a particular holy man.[2] This widow's group were disciples of Elisha;

other groups were known to live and travel with Samuel, Nathan or Elijah. These prophets were important to the daily religious, social and political functions of the Israelite communities because they could predict the future, determine the political structure and perform miracles. Elisha predicted a seven-year famine,[3] Samuel anointed Saul and David to be kings in Israel[4] and Elijah restored life to the dying son of Zarephat.[5]

Being a prophet was not an easy calling. We know from Isaiah the anxiety that prophets felt when they had a difficult vision: "A difficult vision came to me . . . and my loins filled with convulsion, I am overtaken with pangs like the pangs of childbirth; I am so bent over I cannot hear, and so frightened I cannot see." (Isaiah 21:2, 3) And Jeremiah spoke of the loneliness and solitude: "I didn't sit in the company of those who played or were joyous; because of Your hand I sat alone and filled with frustration." (Jeremiah 15:17) The prophets received little remuneration for their work—maybe some cooked cakes, a few chickens and, sometimes, a camel or two. But they delivered their oracles whether they were asked or not. As a matter of fact, they had a hard time stopping the visions from coming to them. Jeremiah tells us, "And if I say I will no longer remember {God}, or speak {God's} name, then there is a burning sensation in my heart like it was on fire, it presses my bones and I weary from holding it in. I cannot." (Jeremiah 20:9) Even though the prophets played an important role in Israelite society, they were often ridiculed by the townspeople for their doom-and-gloom forecasts. We can only imagine that their families were snubbed too.

Sometimes, however, prophets' wives were held in awe, as we read in Genesis 20:7 concerning Abraham's wife Sarah and how she was desired by Abimelech the king of Gerar. God said to Abimelech, "Now return this man's wife because he is a prophet, and he will pray for you and you will be saved; and if you don't return her, know that you will die, you and all that is yours." However, if the prophet's widow derived any status from her husband's calling, she was probably awarded the same dubious honor of being revered yet ridiculed, empowered yet impover- ished. When her husband was alive, she knew that regard- less of the rejection and loneliness, there was a sense of purpose to her life. And when he died, something in her must have died too—that part that gave her life purpose and meaning. When he was alive, they knew that in the in- timacy of their home they could hold onto the comfort of each other's embrace and loyalty. But when he died, what did she have to hold onto? There were no provisions of property, no cause to champion, only her sons.

The first thing the prophet's widow needed to do was the same thing all grieving women need to do: talk. She needed to talk, cry or scream, and have someone listen to her. She needed to talk about her lost love, her inner fears, her feelings of inadequacy and her need for companionship. Now, as you must know, when a woman needs to talk, the need is as basic as hunger or sleep. However, it was not easy for people to listen to the sorrow of a grieving woman. The people in the village did not know how to respond; they just didn't know what to say. Even the women didn't always know what to say to her. They may have forgotten that in times of grief, we don't have to verbally respond. We only have to listen. And listening is sometimes the hardest thing to do.

It was painful to look the prophet's widow in the face and be her sounding board. When she needed a friend the most, many people scurried around with fumbling words of sympathy, offering their services while holding a comfortable distance. They were afraid of being infected by her sense of despair and loneliness. But not Elisha. He was a man of God.[6] He was not afraid of death or grief, life or love. He saw despair as an opportunity for miracles to happen. Elisha knew how to listen to the prophet's widow in a way that comforted her heart. First he listened, then he asked pointed questions. And when the prophet's widow was relaxed and open, he gave her sound advice.

Elisha told the prophet's widow to collect her neighbors' empty vessels and guard them behind the closed doors of her own home. In 2 Kings 4:4 he said, "Go [home] and

179

close the door behind you and your sons, and pour out into all the vessels. . . ." Once she did what was necessary and collected the jugs, then she was to seclude herself with her sons behind a closed door. Behind that door she and her sons had the privacy to grieve without being on public display, as every widow, and especially one who lived a public life like the prophet's widow, needs time to do.

Traditionally, the story continues in 2 Kings 4:5: "And so she went *from him,* and she closed the door behind her and behind her sons, they *brought the vessels to her,* and she poured out." The translator assumes that the Hebrew word *mayito,* "from him," means that she left Elisha, going from him to her home. However, we could also interpret "from him" to mean that she went through the emotional process of separating herself from her life with her husband, preparing to begin her life anew. The Hebrew word *magishim,* which has been traditionally translated as "they brought the vessels to her," comes from the root letters *nun, gimmel, shim,* which mean "to come near, approach or present." With a revised translation we could say, "And she went *from him* [her deceased husband], closed the door behind herself and behind her sons, they *came near to her* [or *they were present for her*], and she poured out." What was she pouring out? Literally, it was the oil, but metaphorically, when her sons were alone with her, she poured her soul out in grief, and they poured out theirs.

THE PROPHET'S WIDOW

They needed to be alone and quiet long enough to reconnect with their spirits—and to hear the word of God—the Talmud says that the wife of a scholar is like a scholar.[7] In the same way, the wife of the prophet was like a prophet; she had the ability to hear God. It is hard to hear God, though, when you are grief stricken. Staying quiet and indoors gave her and her sons the opportunity to deal with the abrupt changes in their lives and to rekindle trust in something beyond their present circumstances. When we are alone we find out many surprising, sustaining things about ourselves. We become more independent without even noticing it. We find ourselves governing our own lives, no longer pining for our other half.

When the widow had poured her heart out, she was ready to fill the vessels with what little oil she had left in her home. In filling her neighbors' vessels, she learned to wade through the shallow waters of her own existence and watch long-forgotten parts of herself surface. It became apparant that, even though she was no longer someone's wife or lover, she was still complete in herself. In the reflections of the oil, she saw her dreams of a better reality and knew that she could begin again. Her vision reminds us to believe that what seems to be impossible, is possible.

The story of the prophet's widow resurfaces in the many tales of women who cope with the challenges of losing a lover, partner or friend. Let me tell you first about Sally.

181

She was married to John for fifty rocky years. When I met her, he was in end-stage kidney failure. John's disease quickly took over his body, and Sally's life. His untimely death left Sally with many unresolved feelings and a void in her heart. Determined to fill this void, Sally spent much of her time with neighbors. She soon realized that not everyone wanted to hear her talk about her grief. So, like the prophet's widow who collected her neighbor's empty vessels, Sally collected other people's problems. From the little pot of love that remained in Sally's heart, she filled their hearts' emptiness. Little by little, friend by friend, Sally grew more and more content. As much love as she needed to give, she received. Giving to others helped Sally boost her own energy and kept her occupied during the day. Lonely evenings at home, once terrifying, began to take on a magic all their own.

They were an opportunity for Sally to spend time with herself. She would kick off her shoes and sit back, comforted by her own company. Sally began welcoming this quiet, calm retreat from the outside world. It was her time to reconcile unresolved issues of the past with her new experiences and increasing sense of self-worth. In time, these issues were resolved and her time alone became just as important as her social calendar and volunteer commitments.

Some women who lose their partners feel like they have been frozen in time, like Sleeping Beauty. However, unlike in the fairytale, there is no prince waiting to carry them off to live happily ever after. It is not a man that will kiss us back into an idyllic past we no longer have—or never did have. Instead, the union with ourselves, where we can connect with God, will catapult us into the promise of what is yet to be. Our future can be as vast as we imagine it can be. The reason why many women are not moving joyfully into their future is because they have limited themselves by their own images of who they think they should be. They believe themselves to be only a daughter, wife, mother, lover or career woman.

However, not all women who lose their loved ones remain embittered by grief. I remember Iris, who was in the widows' support group that I led when I was a chaplain for our local hospice. She had grieved over the death of her husband and reached the point in her process of healing where she was filled with confidence. She was making her wildest fantasies come true. She dyed her graying hair blond and was making arrangements to go, with several other widows, on her first cruise to the Bahamas. Iris was becoming the socialite she had always dreamt of being. Her married friends, who knew her from before as the nesting homemaker, were dismayed at first. She used to be like them, a dutiful wife who rarely socialized. Some couples distanced themselves from her because her sense of freedom was too threatening to them. Several others stayed true friends, but Iris felt that they secretly disapproved of her new lifestyle. The most awkward instance occurred when she shared her happiness with the support group. The other widows and widowers in the group could not understand her joie de vivre. They were so locked into holding on to the old paradigm that said a widow must not enjoy; a widow must be pitied; a widow must show misery. Well, not Iris.

Iris had stopped going to church many years before; yet she still had a strong belief in God. She believed God was a benevolent spirit who, while escorting her husband to the wonders of heaven, was guiding her to reclaim a full life on earth. She used to think that death was the end to life, but her belief system had expanded to include a new perspective on death. She started reading about after-life experiences and imagined her husband joyous in his new surroundings, free from the pain he had suffered in this world. This new vision enabled her to be free of the guilt associated with her old fears of death.

Such belief, whether individualistic or orthodox, can help us persevere. Ruthie was a forty-seven-year-old traditional housewife when her husband died and left her with two daughters and a son. Being deeply religious and eternally optimistic, Ruthie did not become unseamed by grief. She accepted her husband's death at fifty-three as divinely ordained, thereby giving meaning to her suffering. She explained her deep belief to her friends and family by saying, "People don't live and die without a reason or purpose, and it must have been my husband's time to transcend his physical existence to a plane beyond."

All was not smooth for Ruthie. This was the very first time in her life she had had to be on her own and self-responsible. She chose to stay with her children in the small town where she lived, regardless of her family's insistence that she move closer to them, in a distant state. She turned to the comfort of prayer and ritual. Attending worship services was her main source of solace; it was a regularly scheduled activity and gave her the opportunity to be in a sanctuary, surrounded by others yet left discreetly alone. Even walking at night to attend temple gave her strength. She never feared the deserted streets because she had a strong sense of God accompanying and guiding her. After the first year, Ruthie started college and began traveling, for now she had the freedom to do what she wanted, when she wanted to do it. She was alone, but not lonely. Having traded in the role of martyr for one of assertive woman, Ruthie was living a legacy from which her children would benefit. Each one of her children remained observant in whichever religious traditions they chose to follow, and now, years later, and raising large families of their own, they have become active in their communities and have conquered their own challenges with the same perseverance as Ruthie.

Though this time alone may give us great opportunities to see how far we can expand our faith and our horizons, you might be reading this and thinking to yourself, "That all sounds very good but, after all, there are some things you just can't do alone—like sex!" Granted, sex does change with the death of a lover. What is so basic to a woman's relationship with her lover—the hugs, the touching, the caressing, the holding each other—comes to an abrupt end. And what can you do? Well, you don't have to languish. There are some women who say their need is to fulfill their partner's needs. And what if their partners leave? Do they deny themselves their own pleasure? Some women have yet to see or touch the areas of their bodies that they allowed their husbands to enter. They have yet to acknowledge the power of their womanhood and befriend their bodies. Yet, as we know from Eve's story, when a woman befriends her body, she is befriending who God is in her. Self-stimulation can restore the connection between your sexuality and spirituality.

Some women describe this process with the enthusiasm of girls. One woman in my group said, "When I accepted that I was a widow, I then started to re-create my sexual life all over again. I reacquainted myself with my body. I touched myself in places I had not seen in years. With my husband's illness, he became impotent and I became sexually inert. Now I am back to myself and experiencing my own orgasmic pleasure without guilt, without shame." Another woman said, "For the first time in my life I feel sexually free to say no, yet liberated enough to say yes with the appropriate man at the appropriate time. I haven't found the appropriate man yet. But I'm looking." Many women talk about masturbating as a wonderful way of releasing pent-up emotions. One woman said, "Masturbating has become a spiritual experience for me. It is a way of my owning my own body and its ability to give me pleasure. I think of it as a prayer of gratitude for all I am."

Henrietta was blessed with a sexually active marriage. With the death of her husband, Frank, she had to find what exactly would fulfill her. Although she had an opportunity to enter into an intimate relationship with a man, she felt she was not emotionally ready. She could have also chosen to abstain and ignore her sexual needs. This did not serve her well, either. Instead, Henrietta concluded that the best plan would be to go out and buy a deluxe vibrator.

When my friend Frieda lost her husband, we took long, comforting walks on the beach. During those walks, Frieda shared her sexual desires and needs. What she found herself missing the most, however, were hugs and caresses; she missed having someone touch and hold her. When I asked how she could fill that need, I was moved by her answer. She said, "Shoni, that is why I come to your Sabbath services. When I am there I get my fill of hugs from the loving worshipers. I come as often as I can."

Religion can touch us as deeply as a lover can, in order to help us reach out and touch others as well. I recall spending a holiday in Philadelphia with Rabbi Zalman Schachter-Shalomi and the P'nai Or Fellowship. We were celebrating the annual festival of Simchat Torah, a time for rejoicing with the Scriptures. The room was decorated with fall foliage, music was playing and people were dancing in circles around the Torah, which was held by Rabbi Zalman. Then he stopped the music and recited some prayers, and the Torah was passed from one person to the next so that each person who wanted could have the opportunity of holding the sacred scrolls for a moment. As one person received the Torah from another, they kissed it with a sense of awe, and with this same reverence they afterward spontaneously embraced each other. Something that began as a casual acknowledgment of each person's worth evolved into another ritual. A friend who was standing next to me, just as mesmerized as I, whispered in my ear, "This is so healing for people like me who are single. We can't get enough hugs!" Something tangibly sacred was occurring in that sanctuary.

Holding the Torah scrolls, followed by embracing the sacredness in each other, gave us the euphoric feeling of being whole—and holy—in our humanity.

Rituals such as the one I just described help us connect with what might otherwise seem distant and abstract; they help us touch the infinite in the finite. They bring us back from estrangement to become part of a community. Rituals can help a community accept a single, divorced, widowed or married woman as a complete, fully acceptable person in her own right.

Every tradition, whether ethnic or religious, has created rituals for the time of widowhood. Unfortunately, some were denigrating to women and left them to assume dependent roles. For example, Native American women were expected to grieve publicly anywhere from one to four years, depending on the tribe. Some women went so far as to cut the skin of their arms and legs, as well as cut off their braids. They would then go around with blood, ashes and mud rubbed into the wounds for the entire grieving time. They were meant to be unkempt and socially excluded. At the end of one to four years, reentering society required approval from the deceased husband's family. This would usually take the form of a marriage to a brother-in-law. Another example is that of the Menominee tribe of the Great Lakes region. In their tradition a widow slept next to her deceased husband's suit and a lock of his hair. She was expected to offer food and treat the effigy as though it were a live spirit. If she did not follow this ritual during the mourning period, her husband's family would consider her as an adultress.[8] The widows in the Kutus tribe of the Congo mourned in complete silence for three months, shaved their heads, stripped naked and covered their bodies with white clay.[9] Among the Sihanaka in Madagascar, widows were silent for eight months and, in some cases, for one year. They were stripped of ornaments, wrapped in a coarse mat and could only eat with a broken spoon out of a broken dish.[10] According to the famous anthropologist Sir James G. Frazer, the men and women in the ancient Middle East displayed their grief by tearing their clothes, cutting their flesh, shaving their heads. The women were known to scratch their faces and breasts until blood ran from the sores.[11]

We do not see the prophet's widow mutilating her flesh or shaving her head or denigrating herself in any way. The biblical laws of mourning forbade mutilation or any such debasement. In Deuteronomy 14:1 we read, "You are children of God, do not cut yourselves or make a baldness. . . ." Rather than cutting their skin, the Israelites were guided to rend a part of their clothing and dress in sackcloth as a symbol of grief, just as we read, in Genesis 37:34, that Jacob "rent his garments, and put on sackcloth, and mourned his son for many days" when he thought Joseph had died. And in Genesis 37:14 we are told that there are "garments of widowhood"—a cloth that wraps around a widow's body and a veil that covers her head. Perhaps the prophet's widow was wearing this attire when she saw Elisha, and that is why he did not recognize her, leaving her to introduce herself to him; if her husband was his servant he would surely have known who she was. Elisha's instructions to collect the empty vessels was a command to perform an ancient Jewish custom that began when Miriam, who watched over the well, died, and the Israelites' water supply ran dry.[12] Neighbors would empty drawn water from their jugs to symbolize the death of a person in their neighborhood.

Care for the widow was, in fact, demanded by God. In ancient Israel, and even today, she was to be protected by the community. Biblical laws support the widow's sense of autonomy and safeguard her rights. For instance, a widow is deemed responsible for her own promises;[13] a widow's garment cannot be taken away from her and used as a pledge;[14] the uncollected corn, olives and grapes of a field must be left for the widow;[15] and one who perverts a widow's legal rights will be cursed. The prophets often spoke against the upper classes' exploitation of the widow and others less fortunate. Isaiah said, "Learn goodness, seek justice, receive the oppressed, be just with the orphan and defend the widow." (Isaiah 1:17)

The rabbis of the Talmud described four stages of mourning that may have been observed in the widow's time and are still practiced in some Jewish homes to varying degrees. The first is the period between the death and burial. This is when the bereaved are busy making funeral arrangements, staying with the body and collecting whatever provisions are needed. The second stage is the seven days of mourning, known as *shiva* in Hebrew. The immediate family keeps to the house, as the prophet's widow did. They sit on the ground or on low stools, wear a torn garment and do not conduct business. They speak softly and let their friends come to comfort them; they do not initiate conversation, only listen and respond. Comforting the bereaved is also an integral part of mourning. As God commanded Isaiah: "Comfort, you comfort my people . . . speak to the heart. . . ." (Isaiah 40:1, 2) The third stage starts on the day of burial and extends for thirty days beyond. During this time the family continues to recite daily the memorial prayer known as the kaddish. They can leave their home and return to work, but they refrain from dancing, singing or listening to music. And the fourth stage extends for one year, during which a widow, a child, a sibling or a parent of the deceased recites the kaddish daily, and some people abstain from celebration or entertainment.

In creating new rituals, we need not discard some of the older traditions that bring us comfort. As we have seen, there are guidelines within Judaism for mourning that serve to honor the soul of the departed, while being a source of consolation to the surviving family members. Nevertheless, traditional Jewish mourning customs were devised by men who—however caring—could not have anticipated contemporary needs. Let us consider the ways in which we could ritualize aspects of loss and transformation for the widowed woman that neither ignore nor separate her sexuality from her spirituality.

Prayer can be particularly helpful at a time of loss and lonesomeness. Perhaps the widow closed her door in order to enter her own sanctuary within and touch God through prayer, as Leah felt God through her womb, Rachel possessed God in the teraphim and Miriam was enveloped by God in the renewing waters. Prayer is being in conversation with the God in you, while tapping into God in the universe. It helps us feel less isolated and alienated. It is both an affirmation and a declaration. It affirms that we are still alive and have a destiny to fulfill that is connected to a greater Source beyond ourselves. In the words of Rabbi Zalman Schachter-Shalomi, "Prayer is a direct telephone line to God" that lets you know you are never alone, always in partnership with the Source. The words of prayer, and the intention behind the words, invite God into our bodies as a sacred healer. As God's energy flows through us, we can feel more relaxed and centered, less anxious and more tolerant. The void left behind by the loss of a lover welcomes the restoration that exists in Divine love.

Prayer may be in the form of a personal statement, a creative phrase or a chant from traditional liturgy. Some people pray aloud, while others retreat inward. Some people pray in stillness, while others may rock, sway, dance or pace. To know which form of prayer works best for you, take a moment to pause and listen to your body. Is your body calm or anxious? Does it need to move or stay still? Where is your voice? Is it in a song, a word or silence? Do you need to be alone or with others? Consider your environment and your physical needs. Eventually, the peace of prayer becomes a way of thinking and feeling that moves beyond words and affects our daily actions.

Along with prayer's restorative powers, we can design rituals to help create closure. Consider what Pam did. Bob was a Catholic widower when he and Pam, a Jewish divorcee, fell in love. They were mature seniors with no children and chose to live as independent, interfaith, unmarried partners. After several years of bonding, through all sorts of challenges, Pam and Bob became as devoted to each other as though they were married. On the anniversary of their unmarried relationship, during a fishing trip, Bob had a heart attack and met with a sudden death. Due to the circumstances of his death and the confusion over whose religion

Pam should call upon at this time, Bob's body was unceremoniously removed and cremated without an official funeral. Pam returned from the trip to an empty home, feeling both devastated and isolated. She was isolated from her religion, as she was not a practicing Jew and did not attend any temple. Pam, who was used to being in control of her life, did not know what she wanted, so she kept her friends at a distance.

Several months later, Pam called and introduced herself to me. She was still feeling disconnected from her present life and had difficulty planning for the future. She felt torn from Bob and needed spiritual assistance in creating a sacred closure. Unfortunately, due to the fact that they were neither married nor of the same religion and did not belong to a particular community, the standard paths of mourning seemed inappropriate. What Pam really needed was a religious ritual that could give her comfort and spiritual closure while remaining true to Bob's spirit and different religious belief.

I suggested a healing ritual that was based in Jewish tradition. The ritual consisted of three dimensions. The first dimension of the ritual was to light a seven-day candle in memory of Bob. A candle, whether it adorns the holy ark in a temple, the altar in a church or the crescent in a mosque, is symbolic of the light of God that never fails to shine in each human soul. The light shines as long as faith in that light exists in the universe. Burning a candle for seven days allows time for the seven qualities of the kabbalistic Tree of Life, discussed in chapter 6, to enter as qualities in one's own life. For Pam the light of her relationship with Bob needed to be honored both in memory and through the symbol of the candle. Now that Bob was no longer her lover, the candle reminded her of the light of God, protecting and filling the void. The second dimension of the healing ritual required Pam to take one to three days off from her regular routine to stay home and remain in a quiet, contemplative state. During this time she would encourage her friends to visit with her; she would acknowledge her relationship with Bob and, with her friends' help, accept what was no longer. The third dimension was to recite a psalm, followed by an affirmation or the kaddish at sunset, in the presence of her friends. This dedication of light, time and prayer helped Pam to release Bob's soul and to give herself permission to resume her own life.

Since filling the void of separation due to loss of a lover is an ongoing process, the following ceremony is designed to be repeated and altered during the bereavement process. Do not begin this ritual until you are ready to let go of the grieving and mourning. This suggested widow's ceremony is best celebrated in the presence of a few dear friends, and can be a source of healing for the widow as well as for all those attending.

Begin by preparing an altar that can be placed in the center of a circle of friends. The objects to be placed on the altar will be separated into two groups. One group will be objects representative of your relationship to your departed lover that acknowledge his departure from your life and are symbolic of that which you are ready to release (clothing, car keys, documents, etc.). The second group is objects that are symbols to you of a new beginning (crystals, pictures or a gift from a new lover that you wish to empower with wholesomeness and holiness, plus a candle and some incense). This ceremony is for the purpose of affirming what has happened and being able to say in front of your friends, "Yes, my lover has gone. I am ready to accept this in my mind, my body and my spirit and to continue my life in a manner that blesses the past and sanctifies the new."

As your carefully chosen participants enter the room, you may have soft music playing or incense burning, greeting them in a manner that evokes the sanctity of the occasion. Invite them to sit in a circle around the altar. Acknowledge their presence and express your hopes and intentions for the evening. Once you have lit a candle, recite either the following blessing or one of your own: "In the name of the Divine Source of all being, and for the sake of the highest degree of consciousness both in ourselves and in this world, I [insert your name], do honor the Creator who brought us together to love and honor each other. I have grown from the companionship that we [use your names] shared, and our commitment to each other, to God and to the community. I hereby release my expectations for our relationship. I release to my departed lover that part of my heart that he will always hold, and I take with me the memories of an increased confidence in myself."[16]

Following the blessing, share with your friends the meaning of each object you have selected to release. Invite them to share as well. Then share your affirmation for the future by identifying and empowering the objects from the second group—share your hopes and desires, leaving room for a wide range of feelings. When all who are present have spoken, you may want to repeat the prayer and/or recite the kaddish. Then turn out the lights and have each person hold the candle in turn, summing up what they have gained in sharing this ritual with you.

A ceremony such as the one above helps us set boundaries between our past and present, and realize what is promised in Proverbs 15:25: "And [God] will set the borders for the widow"—a promise that God will help the widow cross over the boundary from loss to life. In 1 Kings, there is a another, similarly encouraging tale of another prophet and widow. After warning King Ahab of Israel about forthcoming disaster, God instructed Elijah to retreat by the river Kerith. While he was there, ravens brought him food and the river provided him with drink.

After a while, the river dried up and God came to him and said, "Arise, and go to Zarephet . . . behold, I have commanded a widow to sustain you." When Elijah came to Zarephet, there was a widow collecting sticks at the gate of the city. When he asked her for a drink, she said, "As God is my witness, I have no cake, only a handful of meal and a little oil. I am gathering two sticks to prepare the food for my son and myself, so that we may eat and then die." She sounded devastated, a woman at the end of her resources and her life. Elijah encouraged her to not be afraid, for God had sent him to her so she would sustain him. He promised her that if she cooked the food and fed him first, she would be well-provided for for a long time. She believed Elijah, did as he instructed and was blessed with abundance.[17]

There is more to the story when we discover the symbolism of the settings. The word *kerith,* the name of the river where Elijah was hiding, comes from the Hebrew root letters *kaf, resh, toph,* and means "to cut off or separate," as a widow is cut off or separated from her husband. *Zarephet* comes from the root letters *zadi, resh, fay,* and could mean "to refine and purify," as in the purification of metals. It also means "to be counted in, joined or transformed by fusion." Perhaps with this narrative movement from isolation to union, God, by way of Elijah and the widow, is teaching us not to be afraid when we feel separated or cut off, but to be patient with the process of bereavement, as it will transform us into a new thing, adding strength where there might have been none.

In Hebrew a widow was called *almanah,* which comes from the root letters *aleph, lamed, mem* and means "empty, dumb or silent." Traditionally, a woman was called *almanah* only when she could not financially support herself. It may have been thought that since a widow was poor and bereaved, she was also silent and could not speak on her own behalf. But in the story of the prophet's widow, we see a woman who was not afraid to speak up for herself, to ask for help and advice from those she trusted. She teaches us that though we may grieve over a lost love, we still have opportunities for emptying ourselves of old limitations. Women who have lost lovers say that they never really stop loving. The next love is just different because they themselves are different, made anew in self-discovery just like the prophet's widow. Her miracle can be our miracle too— a very present promise of riches pouring forth from faith.

Chapter 8

Modern Woman

BURYING
A UTERUS

*R*emoving a uterus is a modern procedure that occurs to over 600,000 women in America each year. There are no biblical archetypes for hysterectomy. There are only the many unnamed women of the biblical era who may have mistakenly thought they were less than perfect, and it is to the spirit of these women that I dedicate this chapter. Together, as we tell our stories, we honor the women of the past, the women of the present and those who are yet to be born.

> *The God who made you and formed you from the womb to help you, says: "Do not be afraid."*
>
> Isaiah 44:2

IT WAS a late Friday afternoon, and I was shuffling my notes before leaving for Sabbath services when the phone rang. "Hello. Is that you, Shoni?" At first I did not recognize the woman's voice; it had been so long since Rebecca and I last spoke. I was surprised to hear her voice so distraught. Rebecca and I met years ago, when my children attended the Hebrew school where she taught the language to supplement her income from her part-time secretarial job. Rebecca was a voluptuous, fun, single woman who cried just as easily as she laughed—on the day she told me she was in love and getting married, we were so excited we both giggled and cried intermittently.

"Yes, this is Shoni," I answered, then paused a second. "Rebecca? Is that you? How are you?" She continued, "I'm sorry to call you like this. I know it's been a long time, but I'm not doing so well and I need your help." Rebecca told me she was going into the hospital on Monday to have a hysterectomy and could not cope with the ramifications of losing her uterus, especially since she was only thirty-seven and might still want more children. She remembered that I had gone through the same operation when I was only thirty-nine and that I had been able to see it as a sacred, not terrifying, experience. "Shoni, could you help me deal with my fear and show me how to make this a spiritual experience?" she asked.

The next afternoon Rebecca and I walked along the serene shore of the ocean and talked. As women do, we talked first about the changes in our families, our loves, our work—Rebecca had two children, both in elementary school, and her husband was thriving in his insurance business. Then she brought me back to New Year's Day 1985, when I could no longer procrastinate or refuse the inevitable surgery. I tried. For nearly three years I tried. The profuse bleeding that accompanied me through those years sent me on regular excursions to the corner drugstore, where I (and many times my husband) purchased cases of hospital-size sanitary napkins. I shlepped these huge blankets of cotton to work, to temple and stuffed them in a duffel bag that I lugged around Thailand, India and Nepal. The duffel bag even accompanied me to a psychic surgeon in the Philippines, who relieved me of my load when after a few moments in the care of his healing hands, the abnormal bleeding stopped for five full months. Then it all started again. I was ready to go back to the psychic surgeon for another session in order to avoid surgery, but it was too late.

I admitted to Rebecca how terrified I was, going to a conventional hospital and submitting my uterus to invasive surgery. What was most frightening was the anesthesia. I did not want to put something in my body that would not only make me unconscious during the surgery, but would take my body weeks to expel. After all, I had been trying to live a healthy lifestyle, exercising regularly, eating natural foods and using medicinal herbs to avoid being in this predicament. Yet here I was. I felt all alone. I had no other woman to consult. My mother had died of cancer that began in her uterus, and my father could not remember any of the details that prompted her surgery. This was not comforting. My mother-in-law had never had the procedure, and most of my friends were too young to even imagine the circumstances. And the ones who were older were of little consolation because, if they had had the procedure, they were not aware of the effect that the surgery may have had on their bodies, and because at that time few women knew they had choices in directing their own health care. So I was on my own.

The question I asked myself was, "How can I go through this surgery and ennoble my body?" In Exodus 13:12 we read, "Everything that bursts through the womb passes to God." I had two beautiful children who emerged from my uterus, and many months of menstruation. I was not going to bemoan the fact that it had to go. I was going to honor it and celebrate its departure, as I would do with any long-time companion. I was going to take my womb and give it to God.

I wanted to bring a sense of godliness to what was about to happen. So as we were frantically leaving for the hospital, I asked my husband to call our friend Cathy, who had been in my original prayer group. From the moment I met Cathy, I could sense her spiritual strength. She ran a t'ai chi center in the neighborhood and would drop in on Saturday mornings. Her tall, thin body, fair coloring and soft-spoken style belied the iron spine within her. When I led our prayer group in a chant, Cathy would begin spontaneous hands-on healing. She was the first one who taught me how to use the power of energy in my hands and place them on another to heal. Cathy seemed to be an intuitive angel in a woman's body.

When Cathy arrived at the hospital, she asked no questions. From the moment she entered my room, her words brought me peace. I was feeling sorry for myself, much like Jeremiah, who, when God gave him a task he wasn't sure he could perform, said, " 'My God, I am only a child.' And God said, 'Don't say I am [only] a child, for to whomever I will send you, you will be able to go.' " (Jeremiah 1:7) It was as if in that same passage of Jeremiah, God was also talking to Cathy, saying, "And whatever I tell you, you will be able to speak." Cathy held my hand, telling me how I was surrounded by the light of God. And she told me to breathe deeply, with each breath allowing my imagination to go within. She described what my womb looked like and how it was prepared to leave. Cathy knew how fearful I was of the anesthesia, so she was holding my hand from the moment the orderly placed me on the stretcher, all the way down to the surgical unit. Her whispered words of comfort never stopped. She said, "Imagine that at the moment the doctor picks up your arm to insert the anesthetic, you will be falling into the arms of God. God will be holding you the whole time." And once again the words that God said to Jeremiah came to mind, " 'Don't be afraid of them. For I am with you to deliver you . . .' " Cathy walked and talked until my stretcher reached the door of the operating room. Though she was no longer standing next to me when the anesthesiologist lifted my arm, I could still hear Cathy's voice speaking Jeremiah's words and knew that they were true.

What I left Rebecca with that day was the same sense of empowerment. So often women are afraid that losing their uterus means losing their femininity. They see it as a form of female castration—as if the whole meaning of their lives were tied to the reproductive qualities of their womb. "Just because your uterus is being removed doesn't mean your life as a lover is over," I told Rebecca. "As a matter of fact, it's just beginning again. It's life free from abnormal bleeding, free from sanitary napkins and free to make love without encumbering contraceptives. Your self-esteem is not located in your body. Your self-esteem is determined by how you deal with what challenges come your way." Then I asked her, "Do you you want to enter this situation in fear or in love? Are you giving your power over to others, or are you in control of your own body?"

Rebecca said, "You wanted to enter the operating room entranced by God, not with drugs. And you did." She described how that same resolve had followed me home. She said, "Your bedroom at home became a sanctuary, and the bed was your altar. You luxuriated in the time it took you to heal." She was right; I felt like I had gone through a major transformation, and I wanted my spirit to gently readjust. What impressed her the most, she told me, was how meditative I was throughout the whole process. She said, "When I came to visit you, you asked me to meditate with you rather than waste time in small talk." During that time together, the windows of my room were open and we could hear the birds coming south for the winter and the palm fronds moving in the wind. I felt so enveloped by the presence of God that I wanted everyone who came to visit to feel the same peace that I did. Sometimes it takes a moment or two of silence to remember the miracle of who we are.

When we parted, Rebecca was full of resolve to cultivate that peace for herself. That peace is a possibility for us all. Most women who have a hysterectomy think, if only for a fleeting moment, of the consequences of not being able to have more children, of feeling that they are less than perfect. There are numerous women each day who look in the mirror and do not like what they see. These women may be missing a breast, an eye, a limb or a uterus. They may be missing a husband, a lover, a child, a friend or a parent. When we share our stories of courage, however, we can validate who we are at each stage of our lives. But our perfection does not lie in any one thing—a physical attribute, someone we love. What makes us who we are is how we adjust to or make use of those parts in order to create a whole. We can say to God, as David did in Psalm 139:23, 24,

"Search me, God, and know my heart, be open to me and know my thoughts. And if you see that I am on the road of grief, guide me back to the road of the world."

My friend Anne is an example of how to move off the road of grief. Eight years after my hysterectomy, in 1993, I flew to Louisville, Kentucky, to facilitate her uterine burial ritual. Anne was celebrating the first anniversary of her hysterectomy as well as her fiftieth birthday. It was a frosty day in March, and the flowers were beginning to peek through the leftover snow. The time of year was perfect—late winter turning to spring—as Anne was shedding one stage of her life for another. With a little giggle here and there, friends of all ages poured into Anne's living room. They knew they were invited to a uterine burial ritual, but they weren't sure what that meant. This was the first time these women had gathered for an all-female spiritual event. These women were movers and shakers who were used to being on boards and committees, getting things done, picking up their children on time after school and volunteering for community events. They looked as if they would have been more comfortable at a luncheon for the March of Dimes. That they could understand and talk about. A bury-your-uterus ritual? This was beyond their ken.

Anne, who wore a long skirt and oversized crew neck sweater, stood up and greeted her friends. "I invited you here to help me celebrate my birthday and my passage from one stage of life to another," she reminded them. As Anne explained her thought process before the hysterectomy, we could hear the thawing frost dripping from the trees. She said, "I wondered what would happen to my uterus when it was removed. I thought that to throw it in the trash was inappropriate, and to keep it was also inappropriate." The women laughed, and Anne continued. "So I purposely asked the doctor to give me a segment of it to keep so that I could give it a ceremony of appreciation and bury it in my perennial garden. By burying my uterus I can symbolically continue to give life, to honor my children and to honor being a woman. I didn't know exactly what to do, but I knew I wanted to share this event with you, and I called on my spiritual guides, my mother and Rabbi Shoni, to help me." At this point the women cozied up to what was happening, and the purpose behind the ritual began to sink in.

Anne's mother, who was born in the first decade of this century, spoke with pride of her daughter's conviction and invoked the memory of her own mother, who died the night Anne was born. With openness and compassion, Anne's mother graced all of us with the stories of the women of her family who had crossed familial patriarchal boundaries. We lit candles in memory of the mothers and grandmothers upon whose shoulders we were standing. The women felt as if their ancestors were cheering this gathering. They agreed it was about time we give honor to a uterus.

I helped give the ritual a historic and spiritual frame of reference. I started by speaking about the word "hysterectomy," which comes from the Greek word *hysteria,* which means "womb," and *hustera,* which means "womb consciousness." Hysteria was the name given to the great festival of Aphrodite, the goddess of love.[1] It was a festival that celebrated the womb and its embodiment of both the wisdom of the earth and human love. During the hysteria festival, it was not uncommon for people to enter an ecstatic trance and experience transnatural phenomena such as walking through fire, levitation, speaking in tongues or having paranormal visions.[2] To the ancients, hysteria was considered a gifted skill. It was the skill possessed by priestesses at the great Delphic oracle, which, by the way, received its name from the Greek word *delphi,* which also means "womb." These priestesses would enter the uterine cave of the earth, go into a hysteric trance, contact the wisdom of the womb and return with oracular knowledge. I went on to explain that the womb was the holiest symbol of life from prehistoric times to now. In Sanskrit the word "womb," *garbha-grha,* also means "temple."[3] In Sumerian, the womb is considered to be the sacred cave of the underworld,[4] and in Hebrew the word for womb, *rechem,* also means "compassion." The womb is the symbolic cavern that gives new life and guards the afterlife. Throughout different cultures and religions, burial boxes have been considered womb-tombs. They can be likened to a channel through which we pass from death into the world to come. In our own lives, we have similar ways to re-birth. Whatever enveloping space we enter to seek spiritual sustenance can serve as a symbolic womb. We could be standing in a temple sanctuary, or imagining being in any protective environment, or immersing ourselves in a sacred body of water.

After explaining this, I led the women in a visualization in which they imagined ascending the steps of a sacred temple and entering the interior of the sanctuary. I guided them to imagine that they were sitting in the presence of the Divine and being asked the questions: "What have you learned about yourself? What are you ready to acknowledge about your body?" After a moment or two of silence, I waited for everyone to return from their contemplations; then I encouraged them to share what they had learned and what they were ready to own about their lives.

One woman said, "I'm aware today, as I sit in this circle, how powerful it feels to be female, and how the people who have made a difference in my life have been mostly women—and how I've not acknowledged them. I'm also aware of how I've struggled with how I feel about my body, and this ritual is helping me celebrate parts of it that I have neglected."

Another woman spoke: "I'm struggling with being a woman working in a man's world. This has helped me realize that we are unique as women, and we have this sensitivity to what's around us. We can't forget who we are and we shouldn't fight against it." And another woman said, "As women, we are an inexhaustible resource. I know that whatever strength I need, I can find it inside of me. Only I forget sometimes to take time for myself so that I can continue to draw from within without drying up. Part of this can come from not being afraid to let go of what no longer works for me, just like Anne is letting go of her uterus." Every woman's statement contained this basic lesson: Only in sharing woman's truth do we own it. Some of that truth resides in our flesh, our bones, our blood. Our body is not just a well-oiled machine, getting us from one day to the next. It creates life and holds memory.

Finally, we blessed each other as women, as daughters, as sisters and as mothers. Anne lifted the box of earth that cradled the test tube that held pieces of tissue from her uterus and ovary, and in a prayerful voice, she bid farewell to that part of her and rejoiced in being able to share this moment with a reverent circle of women. That day in Anne's living room, our voices rose in prayer as some recited the kaddish, others recited the Lord's Prayer, and still others spoke prayers of their own. The poet Rilke once said, "If a woman told her truth, the world would split open." At the sound of our voices, old boundaries crumbled. Perhaps our mothers and their mothers and the women of all time were there in spirit, those named and unnamed—and we were one.

Outside in the gentle chill of the crisp air, we pushed aside the last vestiges of snow on Anne's garden. We dug into the earth, conscious that we were in a way breaking through the flesh of the ultimate Mother and returning something to her womb. I was reminded of the instructions that God gave to the priest concerning the offerings of the Israelites. The priests were to take a portion of the gifts for themselves; among other things, what God required of the people was "All the best of what you have and who you are . . . Everything that opens the womb in all flesh . . ." (Numbers 18:14–15)

In Exodus 29:41, 42, God tells the Israelites to offer a lamb with flour, oil and spices each morning and evening.[5] God says: ". . . it should be a fire offering with a sweet fragrance. It should be an offering for generations to come, at the opening of the Tent of Meeting before God, where God will meet with you and speak with you there." As noted before, Hebrew uses the same letters for the word *ishah,* "woman," and for the word *isheh,* which means "fire offering." In Arabic the word *ishah* means "to heal." And another word for an "offering" is *olah,* which also means "to lift up." Furthermore, in the Zohar we read that the letters of the word *isha* also refer to the sacred fire of the feminine aspect of God.[6] We could translate these verses to mean that the Israelites' sacrifice could be given by a woman and that it would be an uplifting action. (And where does it take place? At the opening of the Tent of Meeting, similar to the uterine cave.) Anne's offering—like all hysterectomies—is ultimately an uplifting action. When we let go of our uterus, we give up a precious organ and in exchange receive an opportunity to come nearer to God.

What happened to Rebecca, Anne and myself was a metamorphosis. We traveled from being distressed and fearful of the surgery and its implications, to journeying within ourselves and accessing the spiritual strength necessary to ennoble our experiences. We learned not to be afraid of honoring and releasing parts of ourselves along the way. Did we look different afterwards? Probably not. Did our lives change in significant ways? Not so much that it was readily apparent. Having a positive experience with a hysterectomy won't turn you into a superwoman. What it does do is give a woman an inner sense of freedom—not to mention no more hassle with PMS, as some of the women in my group described one night when we shared our stories. One woman, a mother of one, said, "I was so happy. It was the happiest day in thirty years of my life. I got my period when I was nine, and I had to be adult and responsible for my body and sexuality from then on. Since then I've lived with the fear of becoming pregnant and the anxiety of contraceptives. The pill was not an option for me. Now, after my hysterectomy, I don't have to worry about being pregnant, and sex is no longer a distressful issue. I love it." And another woman agreed, saying, "I had so much trouble with bleeding and cramps, I was relieved when I finally had the hysterectomy. Now sex is better than ever. I even have a greater desire for sex now than I had before." One of the women, whose children were in college, remarked, "My children visited me during my recovery in the hospital, and when they all left, I had a sense of loss, thinking that they were born through a uterus that was now pickling in a jar somewhere. But that lasted for only a moment. Then I felt a sense of pride. I did my work and mothered my children, and I'm proud of how I did it. Now I am free to do for me." Then another woman chimed in, "Now I am available as a mentor for young mothers. I help my daughters and share my knowledge and love with them and their friends."

By sharing the stories of our hysterectomies, we frame

our experiences with the words of Psalm 139:14: "I will give thanks to you for who I am; awesomely and wondrously made; Your works are miraculous, and my soul knows this well." And our voices will give the unnamed women of the Bible a place in history. What were their names? They answer to that by which you now call yourself.

Chapter 9

Naomi

CROWNING
THE CRONE

When there was a famine in the kingdom of Judah, Naomi and her family moved from the town of Bethlehem to neighboring Moab, where they had hoped to find a more prosperous life. They worked very hard in the fields of Moab, and over time, Naomi's husband died and left her a widow with two sons. Then her sons died and she was left with two Moabite daughters-in-law, Orpah and Ruth. When Naomi heard that the famine in Judah had ended, she decided to move back to Bethlehem. Naomi, Orpah and Ruth began the arduous journey to Bethlehem, but along the way Orpah chose to return to her mother's house in Moab, and Ruth chose to continue on with Naomi. The two women entered Bethlehem during the barley harvest and gathered their food from their kinsman Boaz's field. Ruth, guided by Naomi's wisdom, enticed Boaz into marrying her. From their union came Obed who bore Jesse, who bore King David, who was the forerunner of the Messiah.[1]

And it came to pass, when they came to Bethlehem, that all the city was astir with curiosity, and the women said: "Is this Naomi?"

Ruth 1:19

DID YOU hear? Naomi is back in town! The women spotted her walking into Bethlehem with her daughter-in-law Ruth by her side.

"That can't be Naomi. It doesn't look anything like her," is what the women said when they saw her. They remembered Naomi as sweet and adorable. But that impression lingered from the famine years, when Naomi and her family, like many others who were restless and eager for success, moved to the more fertile fields of neighboring Moab.

The women went to meet Naomi with unspoken curiosity. As they shook her hand in welcome, they were astounded by the changes. The hand Naomi had extended on her way out of town was smooth as silk. Now her hand had the texture and strength of a noble elder's. It was etched with untold experiences and weighted with wisdom. And her face. It had changed from sweet and naïve to strong and passionate. It's as though Naomi had turned inside out. What used to be smooth, ivory skin was sallow and wrinkled, and what had been dark, wavy hair was now white and straight. Yet nothing was as changed as her eyes. When she left, her eyes darted excitedly in all directions yet saw very little. Now her gaze was unyielding, and she saw all. She may have looked old and wrinkled, yet she carried the years with the grace and confidence of a goddess. She had the kind of demeanor you see in a woman who has reached the stage in life when she no longer has to prove anything. Naomi had arrived and she knew who she was.

She asserted herself the moment she returned to Bethlehem and the women came to greet her. They looked at her and asked, "Is this Naomi?" She answered, "Don't call me Naomi. Call me Mara, for God has dealt bitterly with me." (Ruth 1:19–20) These two names, or words, depending on how you translate them, can change the meaning of the whole story as it is written in the Book of Ruth. *Naomi* means "pleasant," as in delicate and charming. *Mara,* which, as discussed before, could mean "bitter," could also mean "to rise." When Naomi says, "God has dealt bitterly with me," the Hebrew word *hemar,* translated as "dealt bitterly," could also mean "to make one strong or energetic." We find that Naomi is saying, "Don't call me Naomi [pleasant or delicate]. Call me Mara [rising], for God has made me strong." When Naomi took on the name Mara she was not only naming her strength and spirit, she could also have been associating with the crone goddess Mara; this entity under her various names covered the globe from India to Europe. Mara was the great huntress who ruled over death.[2] Some say she was born in Bethlehem and is associated with the older-than-time Greek fate Moira, or the all-seeing Mari of Syria. Through the years, Mara or Mari came to be known in Christianity as the virgin mother Mary.[3]

How did God change delicate Naomi into strong Mara? When Naomi escaped the famine, she thought her life was determined by outside influences only. She thought if she changed her location, she could change her destiny. But she learned that life follows you wherever you go. In Moab, her husband died. In Moab, her two sons married, and shortly thereafter, they died and left their wives widowed. In Moab, Naomi grew up. When Naomi ran from the famine in Judah, she still had to confront the hunger that resided in her own spirit. She was a young housewife then, eager to please, yet hungering for a deeper connection to her life. She drifted from being wife to mother, to farmer, to menopausal woman as though she were moving from one dream sequence to the next. In between, there were periods of insecurity, worry and fear.

Now, she was proud of all she had learned and of who she was. She had finally come to a place in her life where she was no longer wasting time or mincing words. Naomi had been in Bethlehem less than a day and had already surveyed the situation. She knew where to reap, where to milk and who she could call on to help her get her house in shape. Old friends were stopping by to get the latest gossip, and she had no time for that kind of chatter—she only wanted to visit with the people who had something substantive to say, or were exciting to be with.

She was not afraid to speak her mind and inspired the

women to speak theirs. Naomi had spoken plain and simple to her daughters-in-law as they were leaving Moab. While Orpah and Ruth were walking along by her side, Naomi was silent and deep into a discussion with all parts of herself. By the time the three of them arrived at the farthest edge of town, she had come to a conclusion. Naomi halted and burst into a monologue. She tried to persuade the women to return to their mothers in Moab instead of continuing with her to Judah. For the first time in her life, Naomi felt completely liberated; she no longer needed to be a caretaker to anyone. Least of all, to two young widows, pining for romance.

At first, Orpah and Ruth refused to leave Naomi. Then she pushed them to get real. She said, "Go back, my daughters. Why waste time with me? Will I have more sons for you to marry? I am an elder now, and even if I told you that tonight I hope for a man to marry and to give birth to more sons, would you wait for them to grow up so they could marry you?" (Ruth 1:11–13) In so many words, Naomi told them, "Don't waste your time with me. I am past being a mother or mother-in-law. I am now an elder, meaning I am now a crone. I want to go on with my life, and you, ladies, need to go on with yours. No strings. No attachments. None of that yucky, I'll-do-for-you-you-do-for-me stuff."

Naomi told it like it was to her daughters-in-law. She

was ready to move forward into the next stage of her life without fear and guilt, as witnessed by her statement in Ruth 1:12, "I am an elder now," meaning, "I am too old to marry *for* a man." The actual Hebrew words Naomi used to mean "for marrying a man," *m'heyot l'ish,* can be translated in several ways: "to *marry a* man," "to *belong to* a man," "to *serve a* man," or as I have translated them, *"to be* or marry *for* a man." Naomi was old enough and wise enough to know that she did not need to marry for the approval of a man or anyone else. She was no longer interested in revamping herself for the admiration of another. If she were to marry, it would be for love and mutual admiration, not just for serving another. This was a radical outlook for her daughters-in-law, as it is for many women even today. Some still doll themselves up just for a man, and stay in relationships as they would stay in a dress they have outgrown, because it is secure in its familiarity. If Orpah and Ruth chose to continue traveling with her, they needed to be ready to walk beyond the old, familiar boundaries into a whole new territory. Their relationship had to change from mother-daughter to one of women freely choosing each other's company. Orpah, whose name means "to turn back," returned to her mother in Moab. Ruth, whose name means "friend and seer," decided to find destiny in Naomi's wisest years and continued on the road to Judah, to the town of Bethlehem.

At that moment, Ruth recited the now-famous words in

Ruth 1:16–17, saying, "Where you go I will go. Where you live, I will live. Your people will be my people. Your God, my God. As you die, I die, and there I will be buried; so God will do with me, and more, as death separates me from you." However, as we look more closely at the intention behind these words, we begin understanding a new kind of relationship between these two women, and their two generations.

At first this famous verse appears to be a sign of total codependence on Ruth's part—the thing Naomi was discouraging. Ruth's words were really an individual statement of purpose. "Where you go, I will go," meant, "You're becoming more independent and so am I." "Where you live, I will live," meant "You live comfortably within your spirit and now I want to live within mine as well." "Your people will be my people," meant, "You are returning to your homeland, and I am traveling to the home of my destiny."[4] "Your God will be my God," meant, "I share your belief in an Infinite God who touches me when I am most empty." And "As you die, I die," meant, "As you continue to shed your life before to make room for new beginnings, so do I."

Ruth did not need a mother as much as she needed a friend and a mentor to help her achieve her own fulfillment. Like Naomi, Ruth spoke with unmitigated honesty. She took the responsibility for her life away from Naomi when she said, ""So God will do with me, and more, as death separates me from you." For Ruth, God was the one who created and opened new pathways. If God chose it to be so, she and Naomi would be sources of joy and comfort for each other. Ruth knew Naomi's intention to live without unnecessary obligations or false intentions, and convinced Naomi that she would be an asset rather than an encumbrance to her. Two independent spirits, side by side, they continued forward to Judah.

To understand a woman in her crone years, we will journey with Naomi through her time of fullness and her time of emptiness. What is a crone? The crone is the most noble stage in a woman's life following menopause. The crone is woman at her wisest and most powerful stage of life. The crone takes all she has learned throughout her years and uses it without fear or guilt. Like Naomi, she is unabashed in her advice, unrelenting in her truth and unbeatable in her sagacity. The word "crone" is related to the word "crown"; in many societies the crone was considered the crown citizen. In ancient times, she was a combination of spiritual guide, healer and lawgiver.[5] For many centuries the crone has been interpreted by religions and societies to be a wretched, death-ridden, over-the-hill, ugly woman who has passed the time of menstruation. Just as we may find some translations of Scripture disempowering, so too do we find certain stages in a woman's life undermined by society's misreading. Now, Naomi is our guide as we reinvest the position of crone with dignity and strength.

She was not ashamed of her age or her appearance. Some women are so afraid of growing older they won't dare tell you their age. They start looking at every gray hair or sagging muscle as a prognosis of decay, even though people today are living longer than ever before. I knew a divorced woman in her middle sixties who prided herself on having a long-term relationship with a man twenty years her junior. She spent most of her time in the health club, at the plastic surgeon's and on the massage table, trying to reverse the aging process. She endeavored to live in a timeless bubble, never revealing her real age. Then one day her boyfriend left her for a younger woman, and her bubble burst. At first, she was disillusioned with life and angry at not only her boyfriend, but all men. She thought that life was for the young and could not be as pleasurable if she admitted to being older. Over time, however, she began peeling off the mask of youth by paying more attention to her inner soul. She started taking yoga and learned how to meditate in order to hear her inner voice. She found that when she dropped the mask, life was not as hard and, at times, was even better than it had been before. Eventually she felt, much as Naomi probably did, that it was too hard to try to keep up with the kids just so she could exist for a man. One year after her lover left, she gave herself a birthday party to celebrate the joy she found in being honest about her age.

As women, we should encourage each other to face our own aging process without the trepidation that keeps the multibillion-dollar cosmetics industry growing. We can look at our changing hair and skin and see them as a badge of honor rather than a handicap. Just the other day, a plump, wrinkled woman with clear eyes stopped me while I was out shopping at the jewelry counter in a local department store. She said, "Excuse me for prying, but I can't help looking at your beautiful hair. The gray is coming in so nicely. I do hope you are not thinking of covering it." She caught me off guard. What was I going to tell this woman I had never met before? Well, honestly, that thought crosses my mind at least once every other day? I guess my curious look gave her the inspiration to continue. "I know it's scary to get older, but believe me, I wear my age with pride. I earned each wrinkle, and now that my hair is white, it makes me feel like I'm carrying a halo of light." This woman straightened my spine with her thoughts and the sureness with which she shared them.

Now that we are living longer, we are free to use the time to make our crone years the most productive ones, refusing to stagnate in our beliefs or our creativity. As one woman in my group put it, "I may have been raised in one era, but I am now growing up in another. I never let myself

get stuck in one place long enough that I couldn't change
and keep growing." We are never too old to think new
thoughts. As a matter of fact, a crone is at the stage where
she no longer needs to prove what she knows or explain
how or why she thinks certain things to anyone. She has a
mind of her own and the confidence to change it at will.
My friend Dee is a good example of this. When she was
raising her three sons, embarking on a lifetime of public
service, being consistent was a treasured trait. She was as
consistant about her values and her beliefs as some women
used to be about serving fish on Fridays. Yet now that she is
older, she sees consistency as something that stops growth.
"I've recognized I am capable of living alone and that I can
make decisions without asking permission," she told me. It
is a joy and revelation to realize that I at last have found
someone I can always depend upon—me!" As a result,
Dee is the renegade in her family. For example, when she
started attending our women's group she heard everyone
talking about feminine archetypes, goddesses and the
Shekinah, and after much reading and discussion she discovered that she no longer had to accept the male image as
the only image of God. So on her sixtieth birthday, Dee
decided to show and tell. Her three sons, their wives, six
granddaughters and ten grandsons, not to mention her
octogenarian parents, who were steeped in mainstream, patriarchal Jewish tradition, were skeptical when Dee initi-

ated herself into cronehood in a written statement shared with her friends and family. "At my age I am on a spiritual journey and feel alive, free and ecstatic to be connected for the first time in my life to a feminine image of God," she declared. "The fact that God is here for me as woman is the most joyful revelation of my life." Several years later, Dee regularly and unabashedly shares what's on her mind with her children and grandchildren—not to convert them but to nudge their minds open.

Another woman I know, Edith, reminds me of Naomi—she, like Naomi, knows how to cut the fluff. This is the type of woman who would stand on the table at a committee meeting to get people organized and moving. If there's a party where she knows she is going to have fun, Edith is the first to arrive. Edith used to speak about the importance of maintaining friendships, regardless of whether her friends continued to grow at her pace or not. She would hang on to them because of obligation and guilt. Older and wiser, Edith is becoming much more selective about whom she spends her time with. She no longer has the desire to sit at lengthy luncheons and talk about trivial things with people who would rather accept than question. Yet Edith will spend complete afternoons sharing stories of God and life and love.

Edith has recognized that in our lives of constant chatter and chaos, we are missing something very important: the ability to empty ourselves of distorted views—our own and others'—and see clearly. In Ruth 1:21, when Naomi told the people, "I left here full and God brought me back empty," she was speaking of the emotional distance she'd traveled. She left Bethlehem full of conventions and restrictions and, touched by God, returned without them. Also in Ruth 1:21, she testified, "I have called God and God answered within me, and befriended me," revealing that her emptiness was not a state of deficiency but of openness. Her words are a warning to us to rid ourselves of the disempowering inner chatter that says: "You can't do this. Who do you think you are? You'll never make it. OK, so you made it this far, but don't expect to keep it going. Behind every blessing there is a disaster waiting to happen."

If we let that noise run on, we will, like Orpah, turn from opportunity and stay rooted in nostalgia. Or settle into the "aging process," complaining about illnesses, failing eyes, ears, legs, minds, etc. Granted, there are aspects of our bodies that do deteriorate, regardless of our best intentions. However, a conscious crone knows how to put the inevitable into perspective with a resolve to keep moving forward. A seventy-five-year-old woman I know, Rose, was recently widowed. Shortly thereafter she fell and broke her hip. When I went to visit her, instead of being in a robe and pajamas, she had on a stunning sport suit and arty jewelry. Rose never complained about the surgery, the pain or the inconvenience. She only spoke of future plans. Within a week of her release from the hospital, she was hopping around with a walker and a friend at a beach barbecue. One month later, Rose was flying to a retreat in Colorado.

Florence is my crone mentor as I make my way toward an elderhood as vivacious as the ones I've been describing. Florence, who is my personal Auntie Mame, is in her early eighties, has hair swept up in a blond chignon and is often wrapped in a silk designer suit and anointed with Diorissimo. She has a direct line to the spirit world and doesn't pull punches in giving you advice for the here and now either. One of the things I treasure the most about Florence is her sense of freedom, her sense of entitlement to experience. She recently received her master's degree and is currently working on her doctorate in dispute resolution. When Florence gets sick, she fights it. She can be in pain, and she'll still attend the theater or go out shopping.

Crones like Naomi and Florence are skilled at exuding energy that excites everyone that they touch. This energy comes from a confidence in their own femininity. Wouldn't it be wonderful for every woman to have a crone mentor who would teach her the art of enticement? A crone can do it because she is no longer interested in competing and overachieving. She is only interested in savoring the life she's built for herself.

So it was that Naomi could enlighten Ruth, teaching

her how celebrating her femininity could help her love a man. Florence taught me in the same way. She showed me how not to get caught in the pettiness that ruins so many relationships. Florence knows what she can expect from her man and what she needs to do on her own. She knows the love and romance she wants and how to make it happen: she acts like a queen and makes her man feel like a king.

Wash and anoint yourself. Put on your dress and go down to the threshing floor, but do not make yourself known to the man {Boaz} until he is filled with food and drink.
Ruth 3:3

Naomi was alert to the fact that when Ruth gleaned in Naomi's nephew Boaz's field, she was treated with special favor, for Ruth would come back aglow. This handsome landowner, Boaz, had come over to her alone, after she had asked permission to glean there, and implored her to glean only in his field, not anyone else's, and to stay where the younger women were. "Look only to the area of the field where they are reaping and glean there," he said. "I have ordered the young men to leave you alone. And if you are thirsty, go and drink from the vessels of water that the young men are drawing."(Ruth 2:8, 9) Boaz, who had a reputation for being strong and forceful,[6] did not speak like this to anyone else, but he was so smitten with Ruth that he not only gave her extra sheaves to glean, he also invited her to sit and have lunch with him. Being the wise crone she was, Naomi knew this was just the beginning of a blossoming romance for Ruth. Naomi taught Ruth how to foster Boaz's interest into a lasting relationship. Was this manipulative of Ruth? I don't think so. Is it manipulative to desire someone that you know is attracted to you and then to find out how to touch that person's soul?

A crone knows how to get what she wants without confrontation. She has outgrown the need to come on like a bull in a china shop, demanding that her needs be met. She is wise enough to know how to communicate with her body, and to use just the right words. This is what Florence taught me. She taught me how to listen to the language of the man I love rather than give orders. When I want to share my deepest desires, I ask myself, "How can I best convey this in a way my lover can understand?" After I consider how he thinks, how he acts, I use all the sensations available. I use the language he speaks, a cadence with the rhythm of how he thinks, feels and acts. You will find that the more you appreciate your man, the more open he is to giving.

Naomi also knew the enduring mystery of passion between a woman and a man. In ancient times, sex was con-

sidered a prerogative of the woman. Early Assyrian and
Babylonian writings describe sexual intercourse as an assertive act of women and a receptive act for men.[7] Naomi
knew that a woman who acts out of a sense of her inherent
nobility rather than feeling needy is a smart woman. Naomi informed Ruth as to the night when Boaz would be
available to approach. On that night, Naomi guided Ruth
to anoint and adorn herself, go to the threshing floor, stay
hidden and watch in the dark to see the place on the threshing floor where Boaz would recline. Then, after Boaz had
had his fill of food and drink, Ruth was to go to that place
where he was lying.

Ruth's midnight visit is similar to Psyche's nighttime
collection of the golden fleece. If Psyche had attempted her
task in broad daylight she would have been run down by
the sheep she was aiming to shear. At night, the other field-
workers could neither see nor harass Ruth when she effort-
lessly slipped under Boaz's blanket.

———

*And it will be that when he lies down you will go in and
uncover his feet, and lay down. . . . And it was midnight
when the man turned over, was startled and noticed a
woman was laying by his feet. And he said, "Who are
you?" and she answered, "I am Ruth. . . ."*

Ruth 3:4, 8

———

Notice that Naomi instructed Ruth to approach Boaz, not head-on, but from his feet. Ruth was to first uncover Boaz's feet and then lie next to them. Why the feet? Because the feet are symbolic of where a person stands in their life—the core values that they've lived by. You first enter a man's heart by acknowledging where he stands at that moment in his life, not by wishing he would stand where you would like him to stand. A woman who is secure in herself needs only to appreciate the one she is attracted to. By first uncovering his feet, Ruth was indicating that she would take him as is. A crone knows to look at the larger picture of life and see that each person's life has a particular role to play and an impact to make. Boaz played his part, Ruth and Naomi played theirs.[8] The Midrash says that Naomi told Ruth: "Whatever good you can do to benefit this world, do it."[9] In other words, if you feel you are meant to be with someone and the two of you can do some good together and the world can benefit by the good that you do, then go for it! Who knows how many lifetimes your souls have waited in order to connect!

Soon, Boaz and Ruth were married and she gave birth to a son, Obed, who was the father of Jesse, who was the father of King David, the forerunner of the Messiah. What Ruth did under Naomi's tutelage—going for a rendezvous in the night—would have disqualified her from political life today. Yet it made her the matriarchal ancestress of the future

Messiah, the one we longingly call the prophet or prophetess of peace.

The insight Naomi possessed had its roots in her sexuality. Though the crone was no longer fertile, she was given an elevated status as an elder and considered the noblest of all women because she no longer shed menstrual blood, known to the ancients as wisdom-blood. Instead, so the ancients believed, she retained a metaphysical wisdom-blood, which made her akin to a goddess.[10] Her divinity came from the awareness that everything she needed was already within her. A crone, like Naomi, doesn't ask, "Am I doing it right? What are they thinking of me?" Instead she asks, "Do I want to do this? How can I do it most consciously and effectively?" I know a hefty woman in her eighties who, even in her simplest attire and most forgetful moments, radiates such charm that when you see her you think to yourself, "She must've been a stunning lady in her younger years." Her build belies her ill health, which she deals with by alternating between a walker and revving up the motor of her wheelchair. This woman travels alone throughout the world. She doesn't worry about what others might say, and under circumstances that might keep another woman confined to her home, this woman is out gallivanting through the capitals of the world, attending lectures by intellectuals and immersing herself in the arts. And when she needs help, she either asks a friend or employs an assistant. Even a stint in a hospital or two around the world doesn't keep her from moving on. When I have been privileged to be with her, I've noticed that she did not get sloppy with her energy; she did not squander it to the point where she would be depleted. She knew how to retain her own wisdom-blood. She didn't rush about and was not concerned if she missed an experience here or there. There was nothing she had to prove. She moved when she was ready, and then it appeared as though it was effortless. When I become a crone I would like to be able to say that I know how to maintian that same orgasmic energy in my everyday life.

Many mystical traditions regard orgasmic energy as the life force energy. The ability to harness sexual energy is directly connected with bringing heaven to earth, as the kabbalists teach. According to them, our quality of life depends on our ability to unite the forces of heaven and the forces of earth within ourselves. This union is compared to orgasm. Taoists teach that when this energy, rather than being directed outward, is directed within and rises from your tailbone up your spine, it revitalizes your health and increases your intelligence. A crone has reached the stage in her life where she understands that sexual energy doesn't reside only in the act, and that channeling this energy increases her ability to be loving, powerful and fully alive.

Naomi inspires us to look forward to our crone years as a gift. Granted, not all elder women we know seem to act like conscious crones. They have yet to be open to the enormous possibilities available to them and remain stuck in their cranks and pains, complaining about everything and everyone. Perhaps we need to let go of judging them for not living up to the ideals we may set for ourselves, to crown them instead, for Kabbalah teaches that one generation stands on the crowns of light of the previous generation. We too, then, are standing on the crowns of light of the women who came before us. When we set a glow of sacred light above our mothers, our grandmothers, our sisters, our aunts, the view is much brighter for us, and, like Ruth and Naomi, we can look out over fertile fields and reap great benefits.

Appendix

Miriam

CHANGING
SEASONS

APPENDIX

Standard Translation
NUMBERS 12

[1]And Miriam and Aaron spoke *against* Moses *because of the Cushite* woman whom he had married; for he had married a *Cushite* woman. [2]And they said: "Does YHVH only speak to Moses? Hasn't YHVH also spoken with us too?" And YHVH heard it. [3]Now the man Moses was the humblest of all the men who were on the face of the earth. [4]And YHVH suddenly spoke to Moses, and to Aaron and to Miriam, saying, "All three of you come out to the Tent of Meeting." And the three of them came out. [5]And YHVH came down in a pillar of cloud, and stood at the door of the Tent, and called Aaron and Miriam; and they both came forth. [6]And YHVH said, "Please listen to My words: if one of you experiences prophecy, then I, YHVH, make Myself known to him in a vision, I speak to him in a dream. [7]With my servant Moses, it is not so; he is trusted throughout My house; [8]Mouth to mouth I speak to him, and I show Myself not in parables; but he sees a true picture of YHVH; *why are you not afraid to speak against My servant, against Moses?"* [9]And YHVH's *anger was kindled against them,* and then left. [10]And when the cloud *was removed from over* the tent, behold, Miriam *was leprous,* and became as white as snow; and Aaron *looked upon* Miriam; and behold, *she was leprous.* [11]And Aaron said unto Moses: "My lord, *please don't lay a sin* on us, for

Author's Translation
NUMBERS 12

¹And Miriam and Aaron spoke *with* Moses *about his darkened* wife, for the woman he had married *had become dark.* ²And they said, "Does YHVH only speak to Moses, hasn't YHVH also spoken to us?" and YHVH heard. ³Now the man Moses was the humblest of all men who were on the face of the earth. ⁴And YHVH suddenly spoke to Moses, and to Aaron and to Miriam, saying, "All three of you come out to the Tent of Meeting." And the three of them came out. ⁵And YHVH came down in a pillar of cloud, and stood at the door of the Tent, and called Aaron and Miriam; and they both came forth. ⁶And YHVH said "Please listen to My words: if one of you experiences prophecy, then I, YHVH, make Myself known to him {her} in a vision, I speak to him {her} in a dream. ⁷With my servant Moses, it is not so; he is trusted throughout My house; ⁸Mouth to mouth I speak to him, and I show Myself not in parables; but he sees a true picture of YHVH. *And why not? Are you afraid to speak with my servant Moses?*" ⁹And God *lingered with them* and then left. ¹⁰And the cloud *drew near around* the Tent, and Miriam *was smitten* and became white as snow; and Aaron *turned to* Miriam, and behold *she was smitten.* ¹¹And Aaron said to Moses, "My lord, please don't *cover us with condemnation,* for *we are willing to understand* that

APPENDIX

Standard Translation
NUMBERS 12

what *we have done foolishly,* and *sinfully.* [12]Please don't let her be like a stillborn who comes out of a mother's womb with half its flesh consumed." [13]And Moses cried to YHVH saying: "O God, please heal her." [14]And YHVH said to Moses: *"If her father had spit in her face, would she not hide in shame* seven days? Let her be *shut up* without the camp seven days, and afterward she can *be brought in again."* [15]And Miriam was *shut up without* the camp for seven days; and the people did not journey on until Miriam *was brought in again.*

APPENDIX

Author's Translation
NUMBERS 12

which *astounded* us. [12]Please don't let her be like a stillborn that comes out of a mother's womb with half its flesh consumed." [13]And Moses cried unto YHVH saying: "O God, please heal her." [14]And YHVH said to Moses, *"I will bring her, as a bud that flourishes within herself, to completeness* within seven days. She will *retreat* outside the camp seven days, and afterwards, she *will return as an honored guest."* [15]And Miriam *retreated* outside the camp for seven days, and the people did not journey on until Miriam *rejoined them.*

Notes

Introduction

1. Zohar 2:60a.
2. Abraham Joshua Heschel, *Between God and Man,* ed. Fritz A. Rothschild (New York: The Free Press, 1959), 243.
3. Benjamin Davidson, *Analytical Hebrew and Chaldee Lexicon* (Peabody, Mass.: Hendrickson Publishers, 1981), 513.
4. Reuben Alcalay, *The Complete Hebrew-English Dictionary* (Jerusalem: Massada Publishing Co., 1981), 1658.
5. Zohar 2:23b.
6. *Encyclopaedia Judaica,* vol. 11 (Jerusalem: Keter Publishing House, 1972), 1511.
7. Rabbi Zecharia Mendel of Yereslov, *Darchey Tzedek,* in Aryeh Kaplan, *The Light Beyond* (New York, Jerusalem: Maznaim Publishing Corp., 1981), 259.
8. Kedushat Levi, 134.

Chapter 1
LEAH: FROM A PLAIN GIRL TO A NOBLE BEING

1. Genesis 29:16–30:25.
2. Davidson, *Analytical,* 401.
3. Genesis 30:14–17.

4. Zohar 1:223a.

5. God opens wombs, Genesis 29:31; God sends angels to stimulate people with sexual desire, Genesis Rabbah 85:9; God seeds conception, Ruth 4:13.

6. Genesis Rabbah 71:2.

7. Zohar 1:158b. This passage from the Zohar refers to the names of the tribes as symbolic of different stages of spiritual ascension.

8. Exodus Rabbah 1:17.

9. Berachot 7b. It is from Leah's son Judah that the lineage of Boaz, Jesse and David are born. Genesis Rabbah 70:15.

10. Berachot 7b.

11. Savina J. Teubal, *Sarah the Priestess* (Athens: Swallow Press/Ohio University Press Books, 1984), 71.

12. Ibid., 99.

13. Zohar 1:34a.

14. Sir James George Frazer, *Folk-Lore in the Old Testament* (New York: The Macmillan Company, 1923), 221–23.

15. Berachot 60a.

16. Zohar 1:47a.

17. The naming of Leah's children can also be viewed as her spiritual journey through the gates of the kabbalistic Tree of Life. See Shoni Labowitz, *Miraculous Living* (New York: Simon & Schuster, 1996), 23–27.

18. Genesis Rabbah 70:15.

19. Raphael Patai, *The Hebrew Goddess* (Detroit: Wayne State University Press, 1990), 275.

20. See B. Z. Goldberg, *The Sacred Fire* (New York: University Books, 1958).

21. Genesis Rabbah 70:15.

NOTES

22. Patai, *Hebrew Goddess,* 37, 39.

23. Refer to Teubal, *Sarah the Priestess.*

24. *The Holy Scriptures* (Philadelphia: The Jewish Publication Society, 1955).

25. "I Am Happy, I Am" is similar to Psalm 72:17: "May all nations call [God] Happy."

26. Davidson, *Analytical,* 36.

27. Songs of Songs Rabbah 6:20.

28. Zohar 1:168b.

29. In the *Bahir,* attributed to Rabbi Nehunia Ben haKana; translation, introduction and commentary by Aryeh Kaplan, *The Bahir, Illumination* (York Beach, Maine: Samuel Wieser, Inc., 1979), 80.

30. Ntozake Shange, *For Colored Girls Who Have Considered Suicide . . .*

Chapter 2
RACHEL: REMEMBERING THE
MENSTRUATING GODDESS

1. Excerpted from Genesis 31:11–32:1.

2. *Be'er lakhai ro'i* was the Hebrew name given to the well of living visions by Hagar following her epiphany. Genesis 16:7–15.

3. Genesis 29:11; Zohar 2:146b.

4. Genesis 16:7–15.

5. Genesis 21:30, 24:62; Genesis Rabbah 54:5.

6. Exodus Rabbah 1:32.

7. Zohar 1:152a–153a.

NOTES

8. Ibid.

9. Genesis Rabbah 42:6, 70:9; see also Psalm 34:8.

10. Zohar 1:175b, 3:187a.

11. Zohar 3:202b.

12. Zechariah 10:2; Judges 18.

13. Sir James George Frazer, *Folklore in the Old Testament* (New York: Avenel Books, 1988), 190–94.

14. Zohar 1:154a.

15. Wolfgang Lederer, *The Fear of Women* (New York: Grune & Stratton, 1968), 139.

16. Sephardim is the name given to Jews who originate from Spain, as Ashkenazim is the name given to Jews who originate from northwest Europe.

17. Pomegranates decorated Solomon's Temple in Jerusalem. 1 Kings 7:18, 20.

18. Barbara Walker, *The Woman's Encyclopedia of Myths and Secrets* (San Francisco: Harper & Row, 1983), 635.

19. M. Esther Harding, *Woman's Mysteries* (Boston, Mass.: Shambhala Publications, Inc., 1971), 62.

20. Antiga, "Blood Mysteries," as cited in *The Goddess Celebrates,* ed. Diane Stein (Freedom, Calif.: Crossing Press, 1991), 158.

21. R. Brasch, *How Did Sex Begin?* (New York: David McKay Co., 1973), 33, 60.

22. Walker, *Woman's Encyclopedia,* 639.

23. Theodore Reik, *Pagan Rites in Judaism* (New York: Gramercy Publishing Co., 1964), 98. The name Mount Sinai is derived from Sin, the name of the Babylonian moon god.

24. Harding, *Woman's Mysteries,* 62–63.

25. 1 Kings 15:10–15.

26. Patai, *Hebrew Goddess,* 37–39; Merlin Stone, *When God Was a Woman* (New York: Harvest/HBJ Book, 1976), xviii.

27. Patai, *Hebrew Goddess,* p. 53.

28. Genesis 31:14–17.

29. Genesis 31:14. Traditionally this statement is translated as a flippant question, "Is there any part or inheritance left for us in our Father's house?" But considering the fact that the actual Torah scroll has no punctuation, this could also be read as a sincere question, to which the answer is yes, rather than a rhetorical question.

30. Raphael Patai, *The Jewish Mind* (Detroit: Wayne State University Press, 1977), 144.

31. See Frazer, *Folklore in the Old Testament,* 190–94.

32. Zohar 3:187a.

33. Stone, *When God Was a Woman,* 61.

34. Judges 3:5–7; 2 Kings 17:33.

35. Stone, *When God Was a Woman,* 63.

36. Ibid., 83.

37. Genesis Rabbah 6:3.

38. See Harding, *Woman's Mysteries,* 68–70.

39. Sir James G. Frazer, *The Golden Bough* (New York: Avenel Books, 1981), 238–42; and see Lederer, *Fear of Women,* 26–27.

40. Babylonian Talmud, Tractate Pesachim 111a.

41. Maimonides, *Moreh Nevuchim* 1:42, in Aryeh Kaplan, *Meditation and Kabbalah* (York Beach, Maine: Samuel Weiser, Inc., 1982), 102.

42. 1 Samuel 10:1–10.

43. Zohar 1:225b; Zohar 2:202b.

NOTES

Chapter 3
EVE: UNITING WITH THE DIVINE

1. Genesis 1:27; 2:15–3:7; 3:22, 23.

2. See Genesis Rabbah 8:1 in reference to Genesis 1:26–30.

3. Commentary of the Mharsha on Babylonian Talmud, Tractate Ketubot 8a, Tractate Eruvin 18a.

4. Genesis 2:21.

5. 1 Kings 1:4; Genesis Rabbah 40:5.

6. Genesis 3:1.

7. Genesis 3:20.

8. Robert Graves and Raphael Patai, *Hebrew Myths* (New York: Greenwich House, 1963), 69.

9. Walker, *Woman's Encyclopedia,* 288.

10. Indris Shah, *The Sufis* (London: Octagon Press, 1964), 387. Eve is the Aramaic name for serpent. See also Zohar Chadash 19a.

11. Joseph Campbell, *The Masks of God: Occidental Mythology* (New York: Penguin Books, 1964), 9.

12. Stone, *When God Was a Woman,* 199, 201.

13. Monica Sjoo and Barbara Mor, *The Great Cosmic Mother* (New York: Harper & Row Publishers, Inc., 1987), 58–59.

14. Graves and Patai, *Hebrew Myths,* 32.

15. Joseph Campbell, *The Mythic Image* (Princeton: Princeton University Press, 1974), 294.

16. Nakhshon was the first to enter the Red Sea. Babylonian Talmud, Tractate Sotah 37a.

17. Campbell, *Occidental Mythology,* 10.

18. Theodore H. Gaster, *Myth, Legend and Custom in the Old Testament* (New York: Harper & Row Publishers, 1969), 38.

NOTES

19. Genesis 3:21.

20. *The Holy Scriptures.*

21. Beverly Wildung Harrison, "Human Sexuality and Mutuality," in *Christian Feminism,* ed. Judith L. Weidman (New York: Harper & Row Publishers, 1984), 147–48.

22. Sjoo and Mor, *Great Cosmic Mother,* 264.

23. Zohar 1:50a.

24. Zohar 3:81b.

Chapter 4
JOCHEBED: BIRTHING MOTHERHOOD

1. Excerpted from Exodus 1:1–10.

2. Sir E. A. Wallis Budge, *Gods of the Egyptians,* vol. 1 (New York: Dover, 1969), 487.

3. Otto Rank, *The Myth of the Birth of the Hero* (New York: Vintage Books, 1959), 18–19.

4. Genesis 37:23–29.

5. Genesis 39–49.

6. Sotah 12a.

7. Zohar 2:19a.

8. Numbers 26:59; Babylonian Talmud, Tractate Bava Batra 120a.

9. Exodus 1:15.

10. Ecclesiastes Rabbah 7:3.

11. Three patrons; a term used to indicate Miriam, Aaron and Moses, in Songs of Songs Rabbah 4:14.

12. Zohar 2:190b; Song of Songs Rabbah 4:14.

13. Zohar 1:29b.

14. Exodus Rabbah 1:22.
15. Exodus 1:19.
16. Numbers Rabbah 3:6.
17. Kiddushin 30b.

Chapter 5
DEBORAH: BIRTHING A WOMAN'S LIFE

1. Judges 4 and 5.
2. Judges 5:6.
3. *Yalkut Shimoni,* Judges 42.
4. Babylonian Talmud, Tractate Rosh Hashanah 16b.
5. Davidson, *Analytical,* 575.
6. Midrash Abba Guryon 3.
7. Pesachim 118b.
8. Zohar 1:32b.
9. Ibid.
10. Ruth Rabbah 1:1.
11. Davidson, *Analytical,* 330.
12. Targum Shoftim 4:5.
13. Norma Lorre Goodrich, *Priestesses* (New York: Harper-Collins, 1989), 32, 38.
14. Walker, *Woman's Encyclopedia,* 407.
15. Ibid., 408.
16. The nymphs that officiated at marriages and controlled honeymoons were also called hymens. Some say that the bees flying now are the souls of the nymphs who once served Aphrodite. See Barbara G. Walker, *The Woman's Dictionary of Symbols and Sacred Objects* (San Francisco: HarperCollins, 1988), 414–15.

17. Labowitz, *Miraculous Living*. For a further understanding of Ezekiel's vision see 43–47.

18. Leviticus 26:15–18.

19. Babylonian Talmud, Tractate Megillah 14a.

20. Targum Shoftim 4:5.

21. Seder Eliyahu Rabbah 10.

22. Pesachim 66b.

23. Zohar 1:164a.

24. Joshua 8:3.

25. Judges 8:21.

26. 1 Samuel 9:26.

27. 1 Samuel 18:27.

Chapter 6
MIRIAM: CHANGING SEASONS

1. Numbers 12:1–15. Please refer to appendix for a more detailed version of this biblical text and author's retranslation than is presented in the chapter.

2. This was not unusual; in Exodus 4:19 and Exodus 4:27 we learn that Aaron and Moses could hear each other and God simultaneously. When Moses heard God say "return to Egypt," Aaron heard "go into the desert to meet Moses." Exodus Rabbah 5:9.

3. Exodus Rabbah 1:26.

4. Exodus 25:22. "There I will meet you and speak with you [from between the cherubim's wings]."

5. Zohar 2:152b.

6. Numbers 12:2.

7. The cloud of God, known as the cloud of Glory, is said to have waited for Miriam. Shocher Tov 15:4.

8. Zohar 2:19a.

9. Avot 1:12.

10. Davidson, *Analytical,* 310.

11. Ibid., 651; Marcus Jastrow, *A Dictionary* (New York: The Judaica Press, Inc., 1989), 1303.

12. Genesis Rabbah 88:5; Miriam's Well produced blossoms and fruit in the desert. Song of Songs Rabbah 4:28.

13. Avot 1:12.

14. Exodus Rabbah 1:13; Pesikta Rabbati 43:27.

15. Exodus Rabbah 1:13.

16. Pesikta Rabbati 43:27.

17. Zohar 3, p. 163a.

18. Sir E. A. Wallis Budge, *Egyptian Language* (New York: Dover Publications, 1983), 76.

19. 1 Chronicles 4:5.

20. 1 Chronicles 4:8; Exodus Rabbah 1:17.

21. For a discussion of the kabbalistic qualities of God see Labowitz, *Miraculous Living.*

22. Temurah 16a.

23. Leviticus Rabbah 22:4.

24. Leviticus Rabbah 22:4.

25. Numbers Rabbah 1:4.

26. Numbers Rabbah 1:2.

27. Exodus 15:21.

Chapter 7
THE PROPHET'S WIDOW: FROM EMPTY TO FULL

1. 2 Kings 4:1–7.
2. See 1 Samuel 10:5, 10; 2 Kings 4:38; 2 Kings 2:3, 5, 7, 15.
3. 2 Kings 8:1.
4. 1 Samuel 9, 16.
5. 1 Kings 17: 17–24.
6. 2 Kings 4:9.
7. Shevuot 30b.
8. Carolyn Niethammer, *Daughters of the Earth* (New York: Macmillan Publishers, 1977), 99–101.
9. Frazer, *Folk-Lore in the Old Testament* (1923), 343.
10. Ibid., 344.
11. Ibid., 379.
12. Numbers 30:10.
13. Deuteronomy 24:17.
14. Deuteronomy 24:18–21.
15. Numbers 20:2.
16. This blessing was inspired by Tirzah Firestone's article "Healing the Jewish Divorce Ceremony and Ourselves," in *New Menorah,* 2d series: No. 25, Rosh Hashanah 5752, Philadelphia.
17. 1 Kings 17:1–16.

Chapter 8
MODERN WOMAN: BURYING A UTERUS

1. Walker, *Woman's Dictionary,* 330; *Woman's Encyclopedia,* 218.
2. Sjoo and Mor, *Great Cosmic Mother,* 190.

259

NOTES

3. Campbell, Joseph, *The Masks of God: Creative Mythology* (New York: Penguin Books, 1976), 168.

4. Walker, *Woman's Dictionary,* 330–31.

5. The Hebrew word for lamb, *keves,* uses the same basic Hebrew letters as the word *kevesh,* meaning "to ascend." Perhaps God was telling the Israelites that, rather than offering animals, they could sacrifice, or make sacred, their thoughts by lifting them to higher levels of awareness and action.

6. Zohar 1:49a.

Chapter 9
NAOMI: CROWNING THE CRONE

1. Ruth 1:1–4.

2. Walker, *Woman's Encyclopedia,* 581.

3. J. J. Bachofen, *Myth, Religion and Mother Right* (Princeton: Princeton University Press, 1967), 57.

4. Ruth had a destiny to fulfill. She was the ancestor of King David, who was the forerunner of the Messiah.

5. Barbara G. Walker, *The Crone* (San Francisco: Harper & Row, 1985), 14.

6. Ruth 2:1.

7. *Assyrian and Babylonian Literature, Selected Translations* (New York: D. Appleton & Co., 1901), 338–39, as cited in Walker, *Crone,* 17–18.

8. Ruth Rabbah 7:7.

9. Ruth Rabbah 2:24.

10. Walker, *Crone,* 49.

Index

INDEX

INDEX

INDEX

INDEX

INDEX

INDEX

INDEX

INDEX

About the Author

Shoni Labowitz is a nationally known lecturer, spiritual guide and creator of healing rituals in the Jewish kabbalistic tradition. She is the director of Living Waters, a spiritual health spa program, and is co-rabbi with her husband, Phillip Labowitz, of Temple Adath Or in Fort Lauderdale. Her e-mail address is *shonilabowitz@mindspring.com.* This is her second book.